AF408401

Where's Chad?
Ralphy Coleman

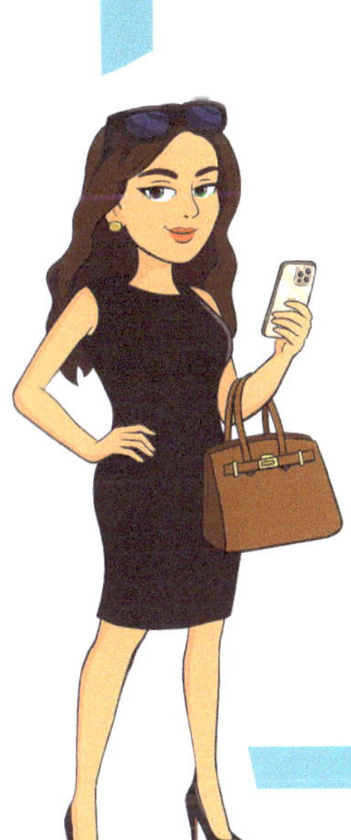

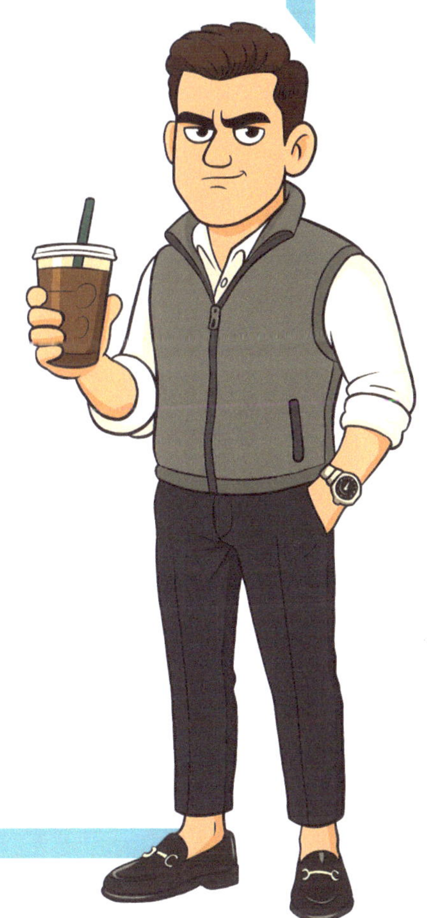

Where's Chad?
Copyright © 2025 by Where's Chad LLC

Trademarks
"WHERE'S CHAD?", "CHAD," and "BECKY" are trademarks of Where's Chad LLC. All rights reserved. All other trademarks, logos, and brand names are the property of their respective owners and are used herein for parody, commentary, or identification purposes only.

Author: Ralphy Coleman
ISBN (Hardback): 979-8-9933464-0-3
ISBN (Paperback): 979-8-9933464-1-0

Published by Where's Chad LLC
1023 E Lincolnway
Cheyenne, WY 82001

Printed in the United States of America

Parody Disclaimer
This book is a work of parody and satire. All characters, scenes, and references are fictionalized for humorous purposes. Any resemblance to actual persons, living or dead, or to real companies, brands, or institutions, is purely coincidental or used in a parodic manner. No endorsement, sponsorship, or affiliation is implied.

Dedication

For every finance bro still refreshing Bloomberg at 2 a.m.

For every Becky who ghosted him anyway.

This one's for you.

Contents

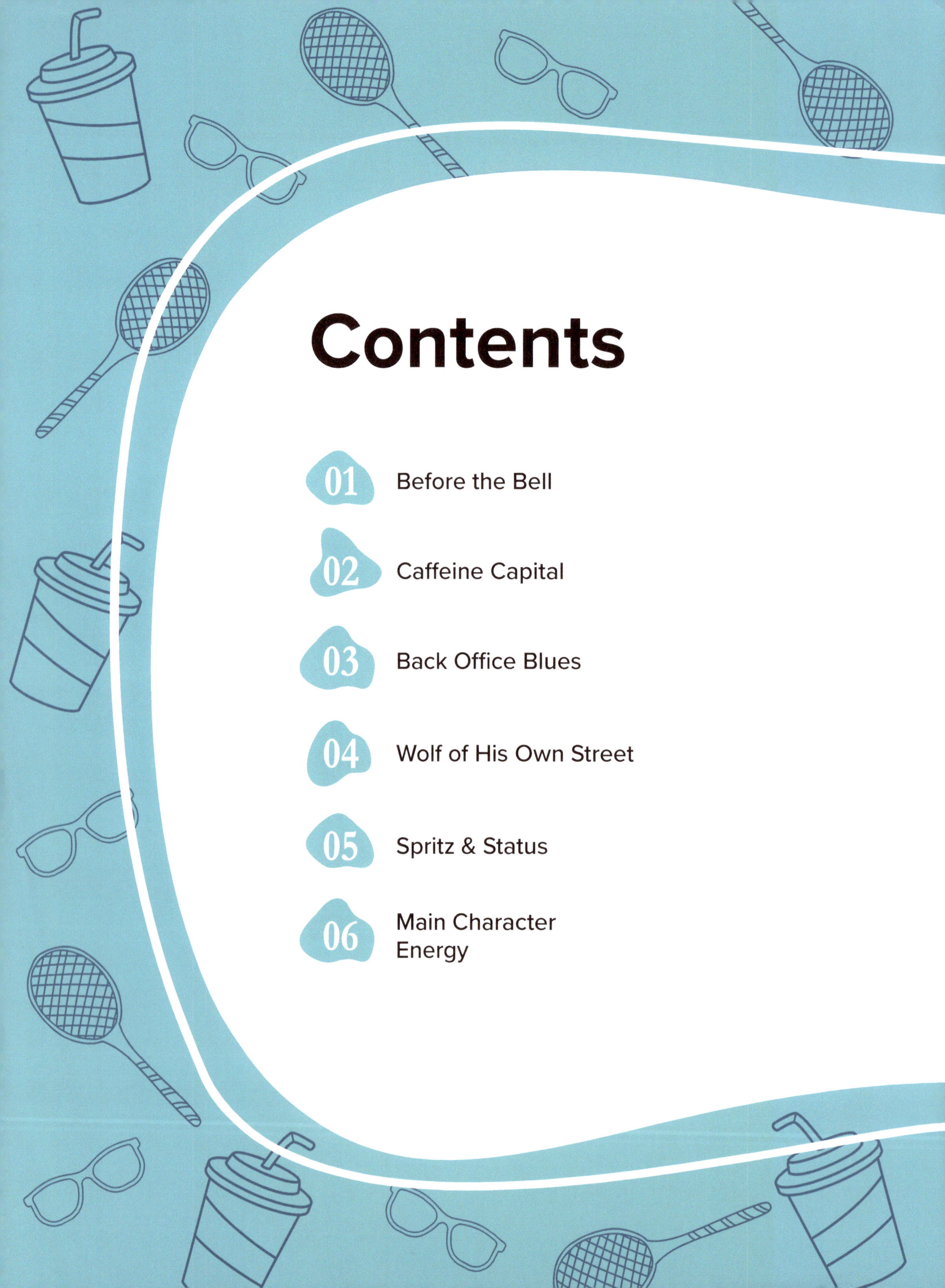

01 Before the Bell

02 Caffeine Capital

03 Back Office Blues

04 Wolf of His Own Street

05 Spritz & Status

06 Main Character Energy

Contents

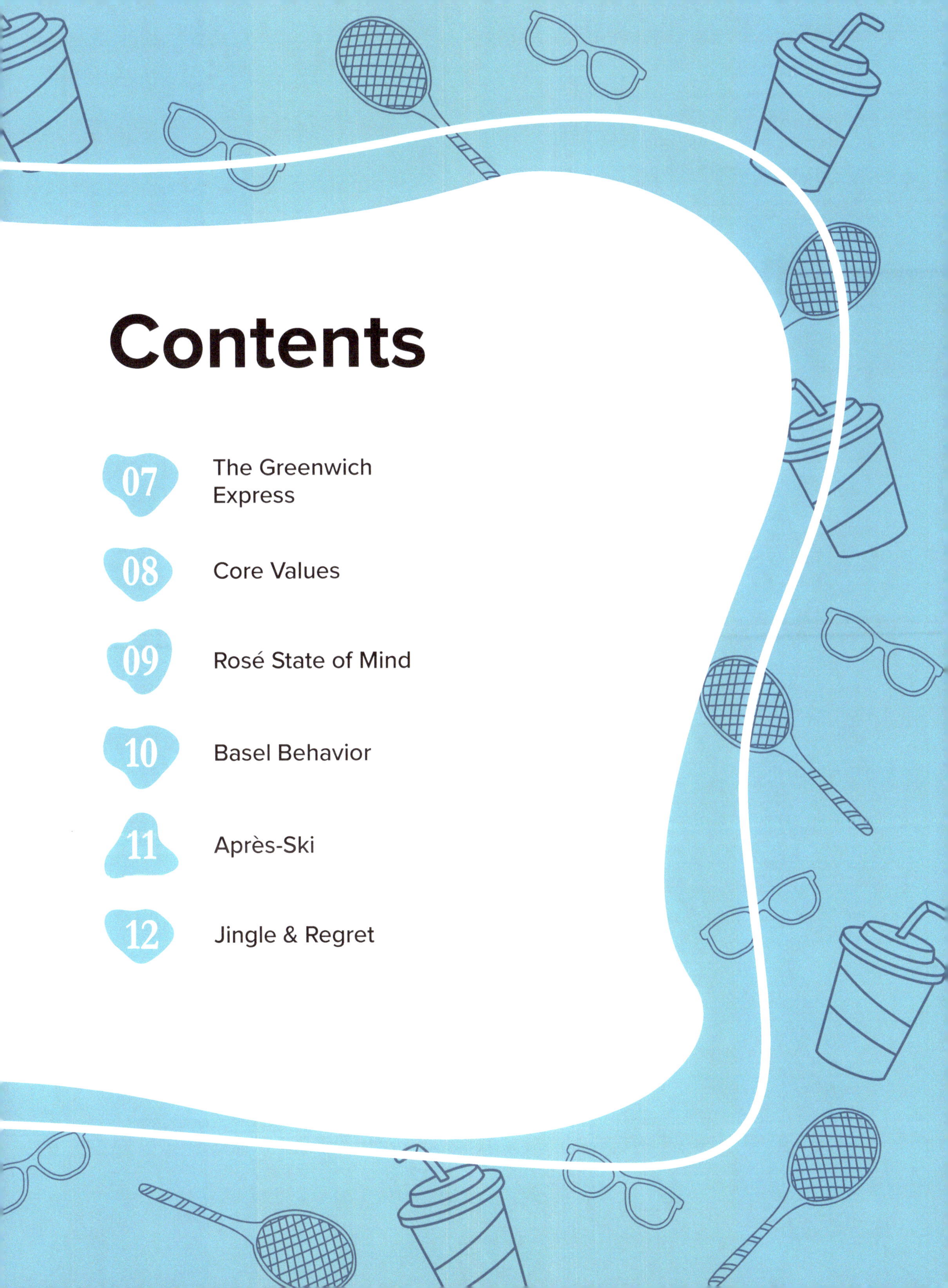

07 — The Greenwich Express

08 — Core Values

09 — Rosé State of Mind

10 — Basel Behavior

11 — Après-Ski

12 — Jingle & Regret

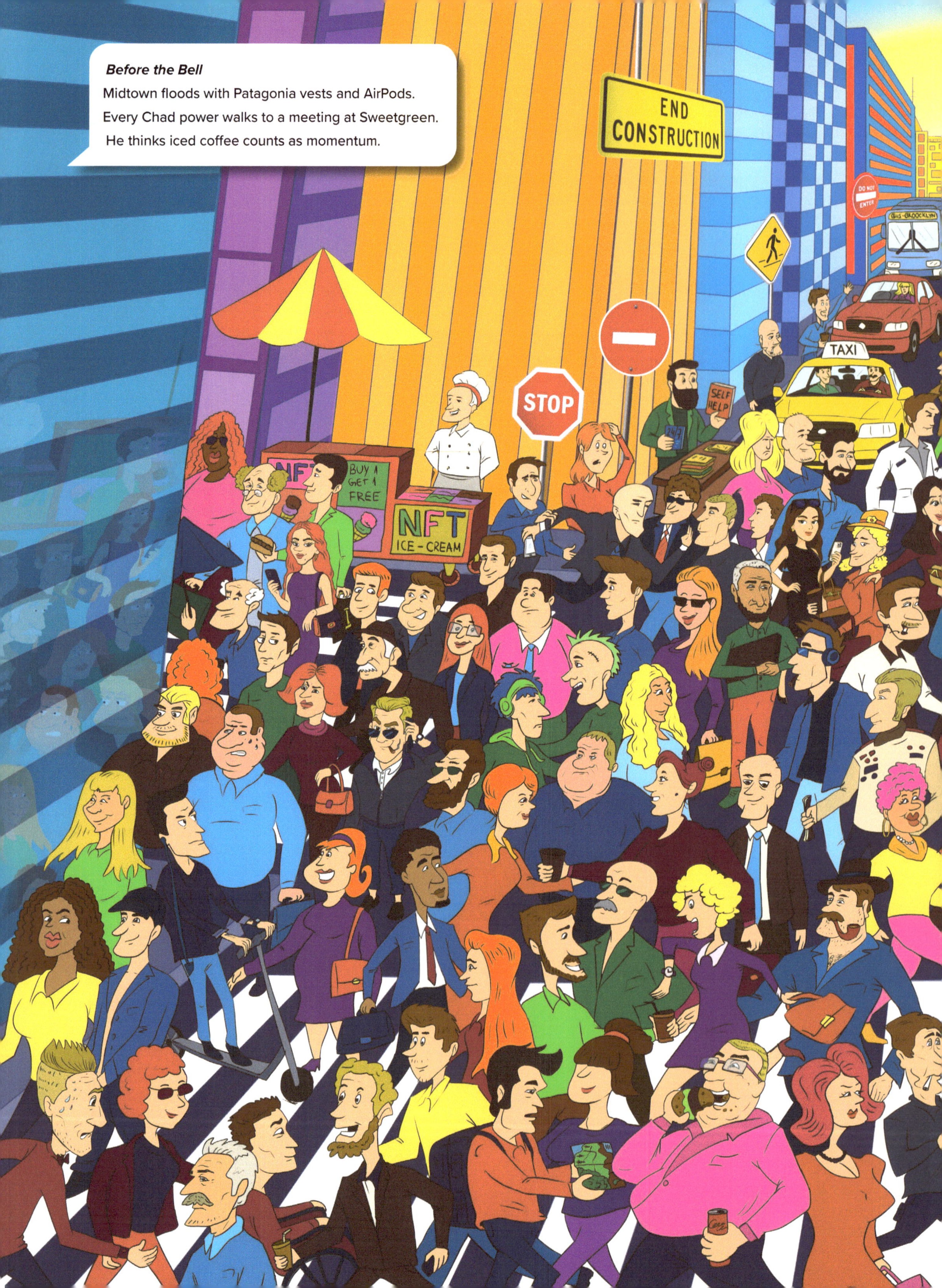

Before the Bell
Midtown floods with Patagonia vests and AirPods.
Every Chad power walks to a meeting at Sweetgreen.
He thinks iced coffee counts as momentum.
END CONSTRUCTION
DO NOT ENTER
TAXI
STOP
SELF HELP
NFT
BUY A GET 1 FREE
NFT ICE-CREAM

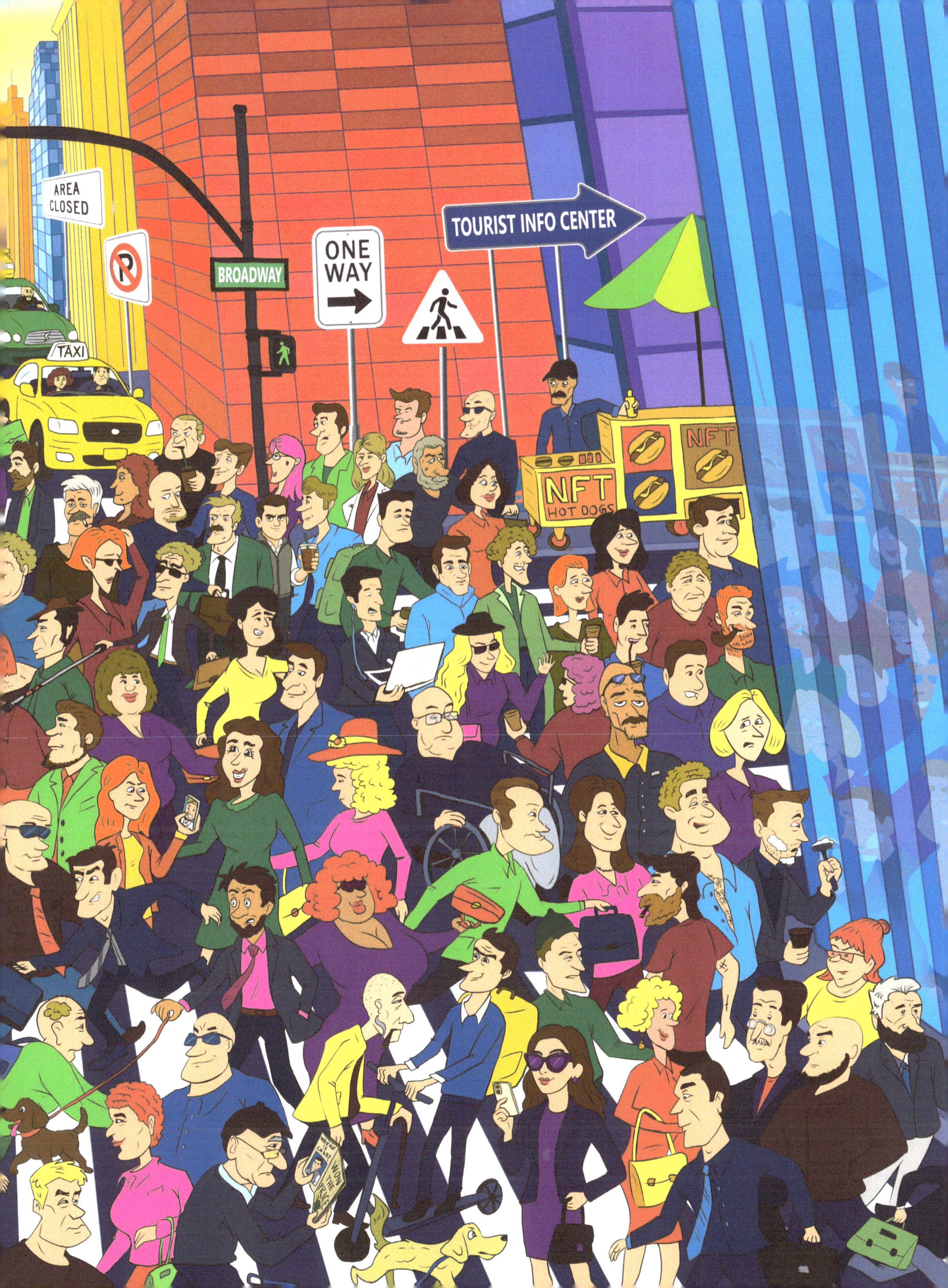
AREA CLOSED
TAXI
BROADWAY
ONE WAY
TOURIST INFO CENTER
NFT HOT DOGS
NFT

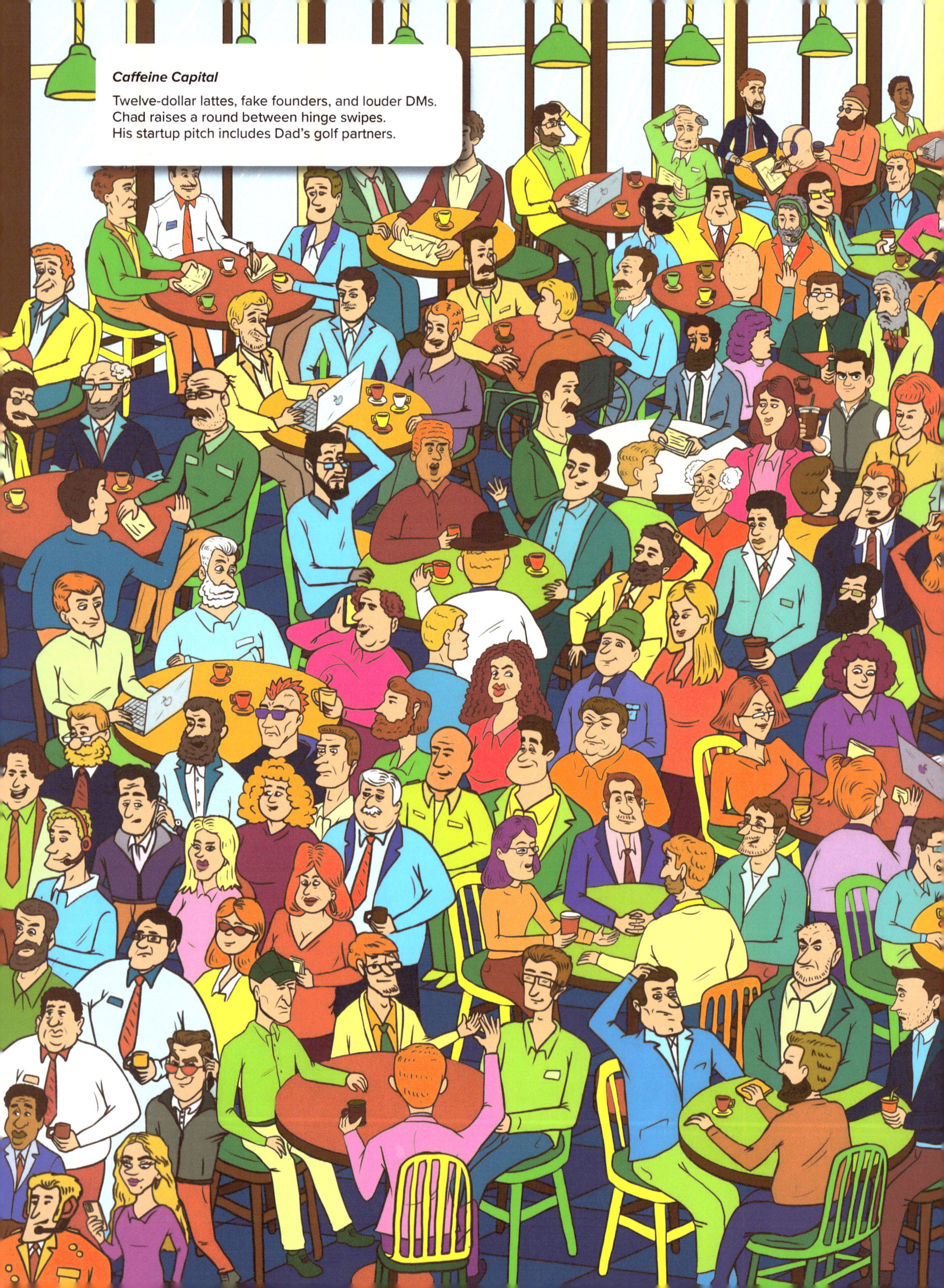

Caffeine Capital
Twelve-dollar lattes, fake founders, and louder DMs.
Chad raises a round between hinge swipes.
His startup pitch includes Dad's golf partners.

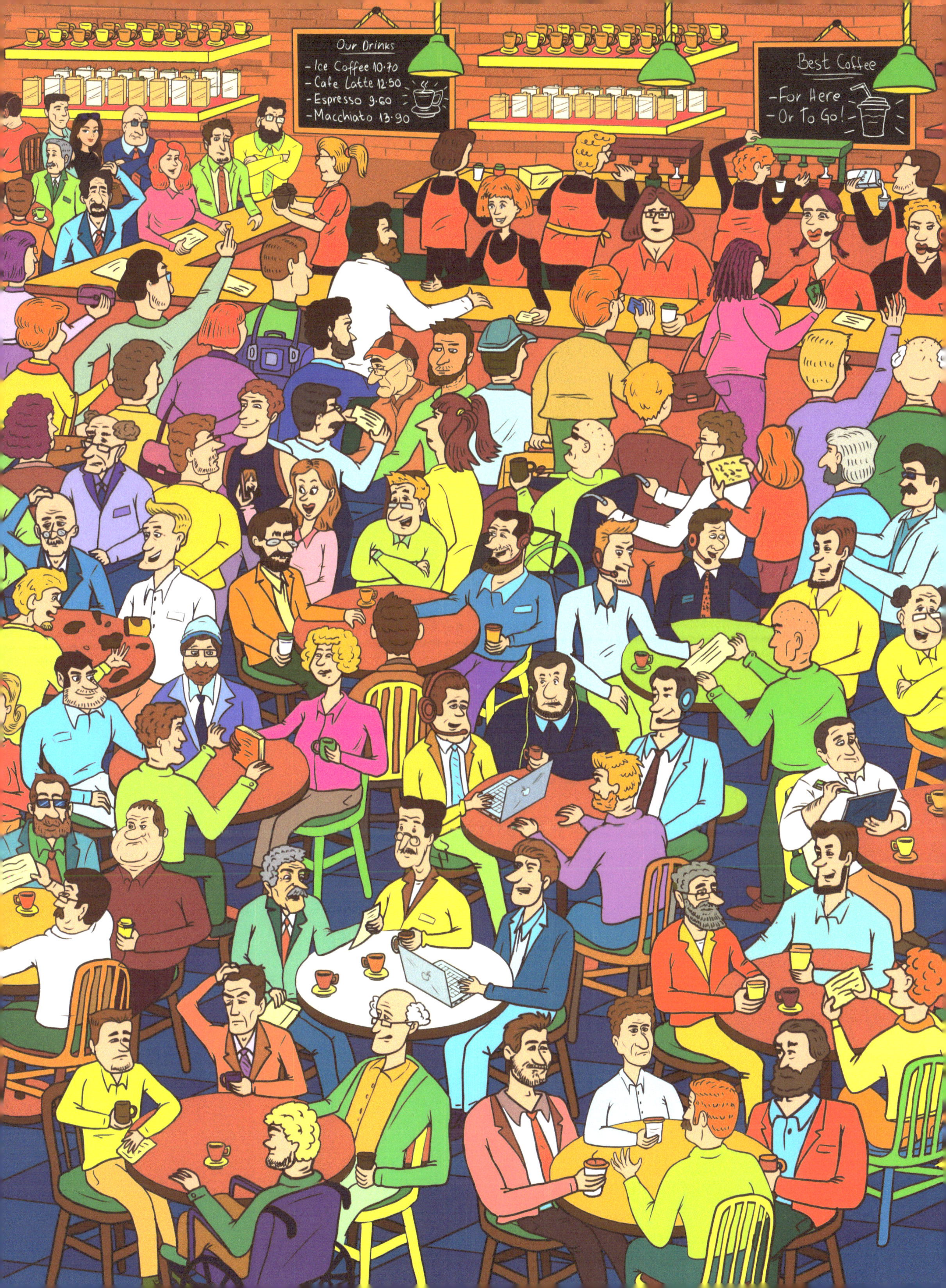

Our Drinks
- Ice Coffee 10·70
- Cafe Latte 12·50
- Espresso 9·60
- Macchiato 13·90
Best Coffee
- For Here
- Or To Go!

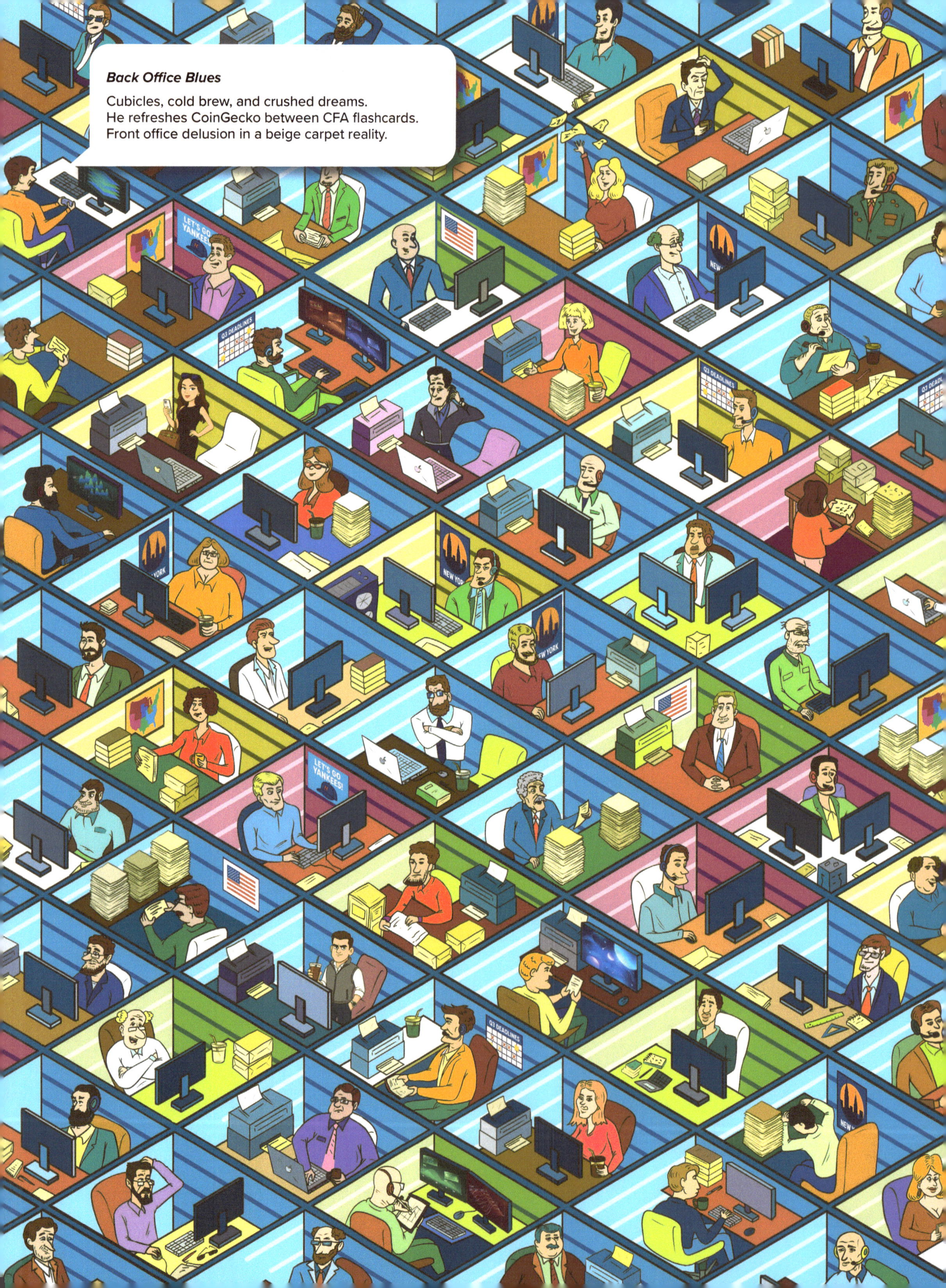

Back Office Blues
Cubicles, cold brew, and crushed dreams.
He refreshes CoinGecko between CFA flashcards.
Front office delusion in a beige carpet reality.

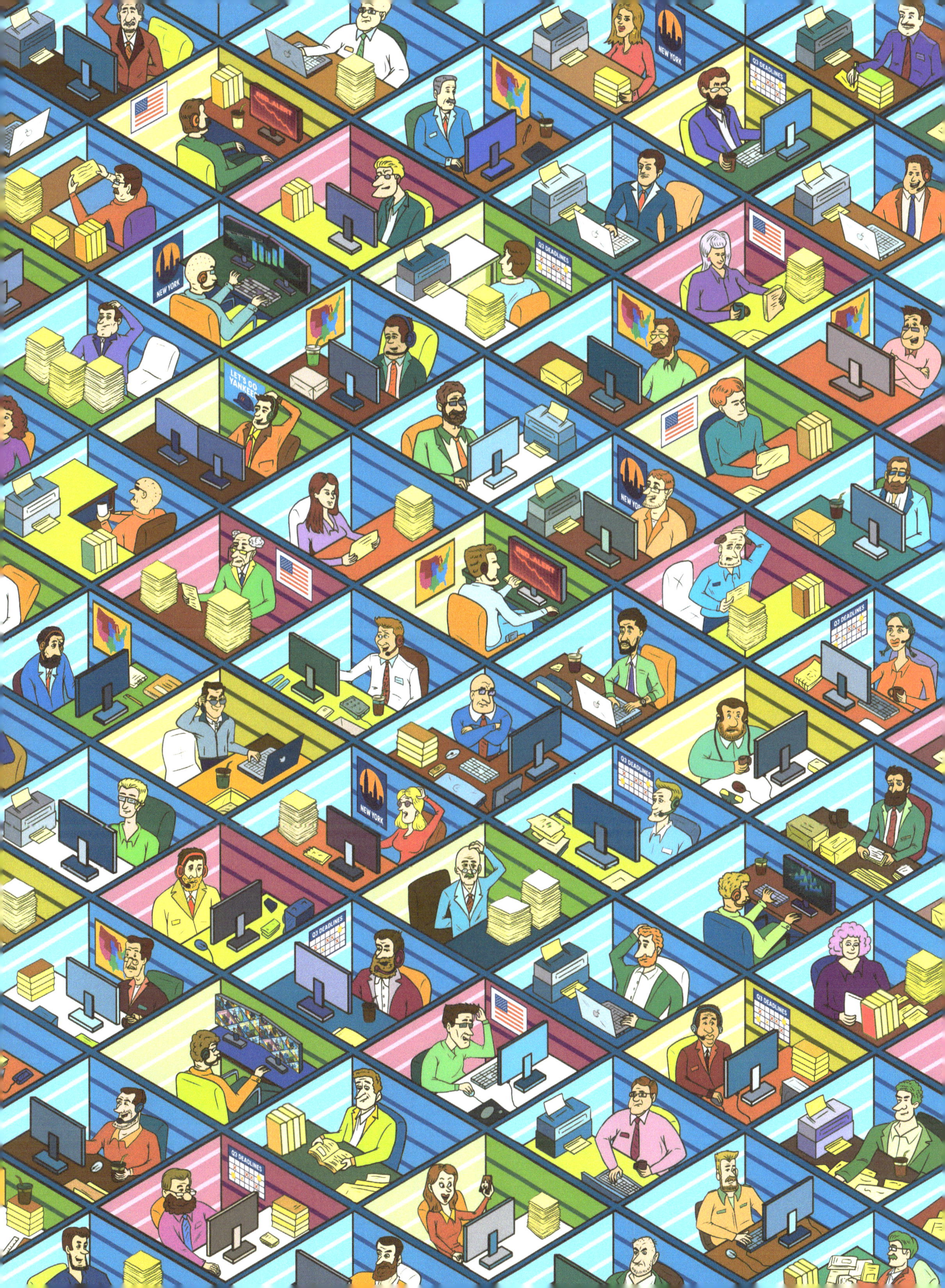

NEW YORK
Q3 DEADLINES
RED ALERT
NEW YORK
LET'S GO YANKEES
Q3 DEADLINES
NEW YORK
RED ALERT
Q3 DEADLINES
NEW YORK
Q3 DEADLINES
Q3 DEADLINES
Q3 DEADLINES

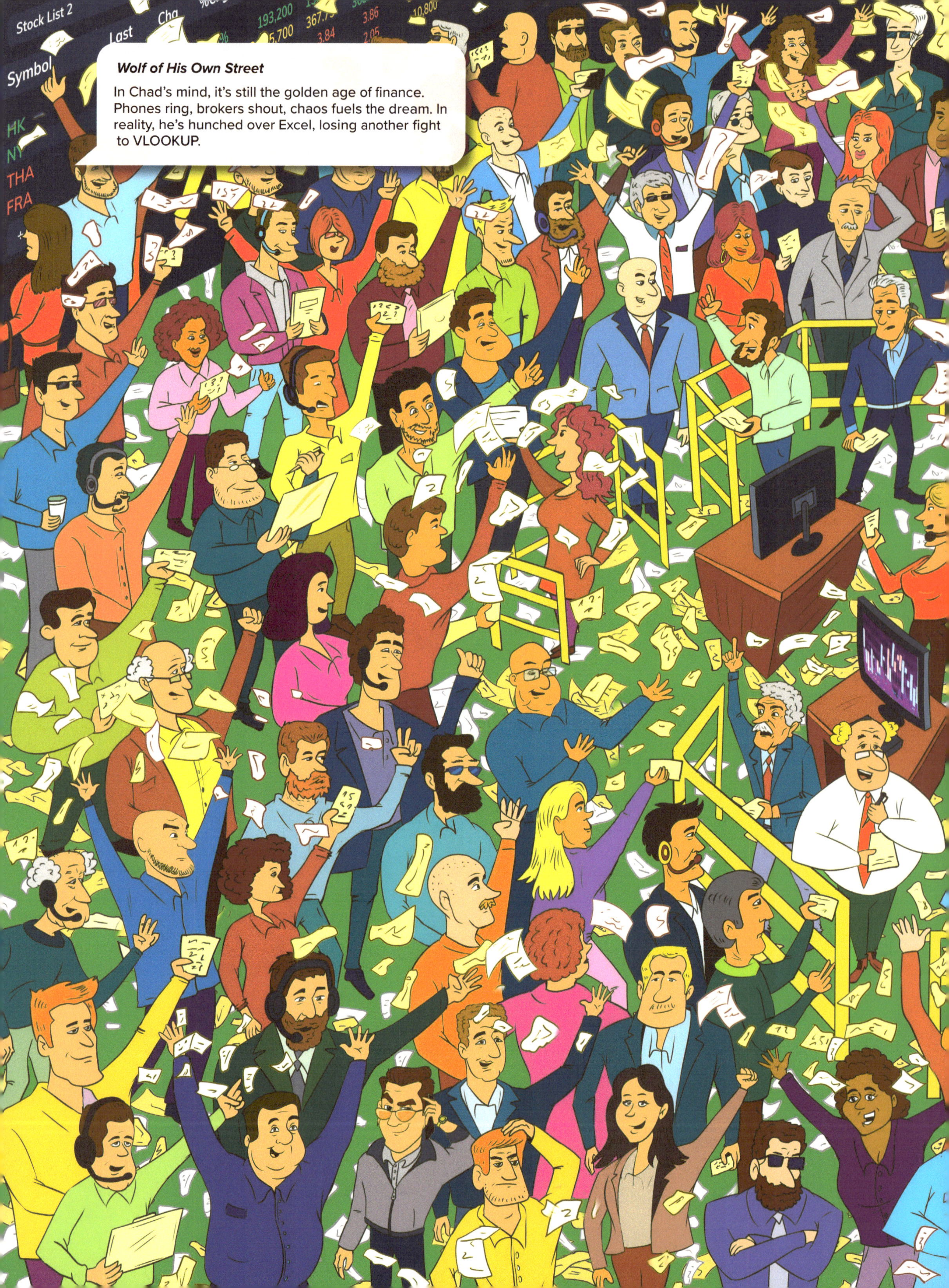

Stock List 2
Last
Cha
Symbol
HK
NY
THA
FRA
193,200
367,
5,700
3,84
3,86
2,05
10,800
Wolf of His Own Street
In Chad's mind, it's still the golden age of finance. Phones ring, brokers shout, chaos fuels the dream. In reality, he's hunched over Excel, losing another fight to VLOOKUP.

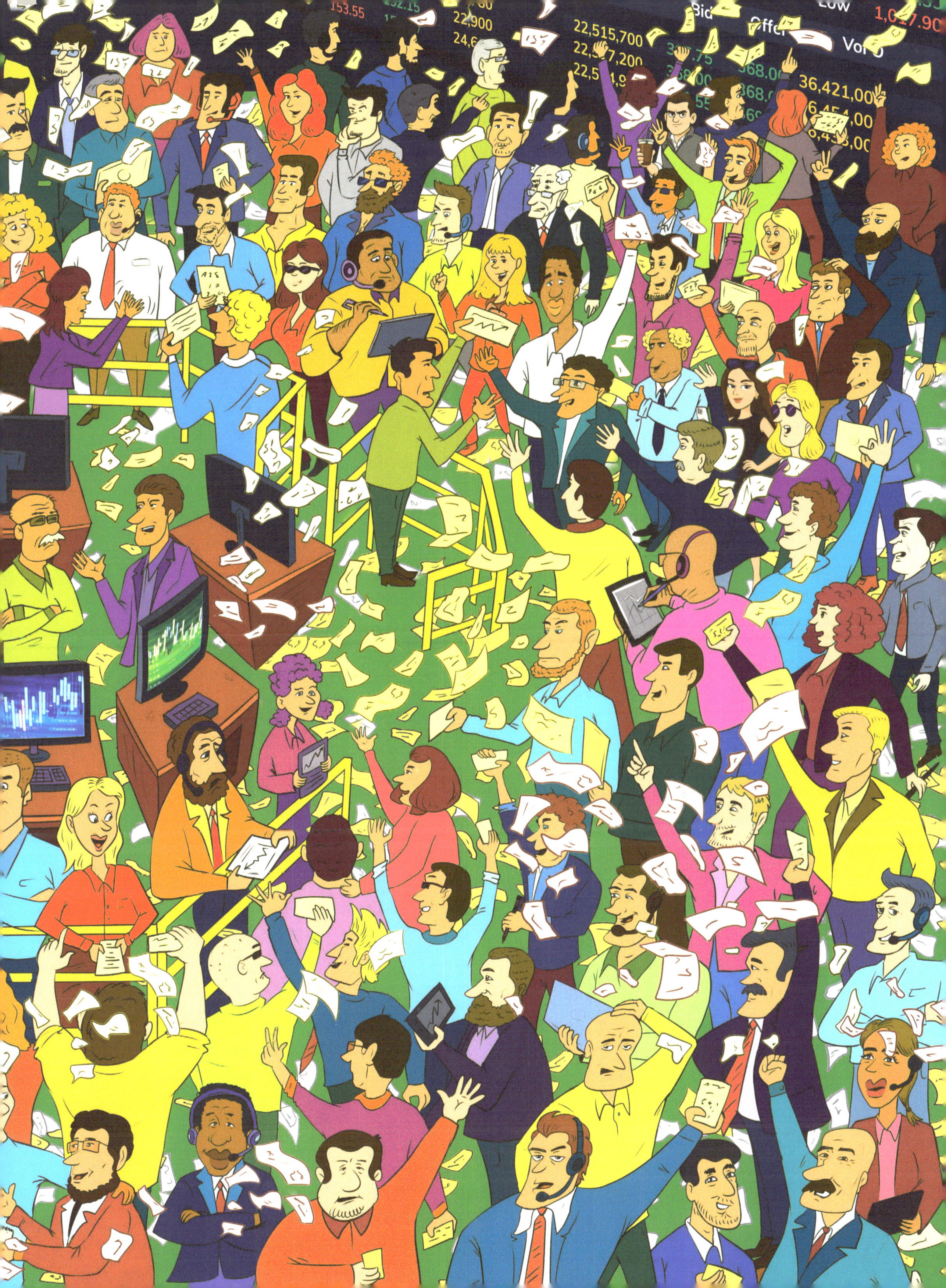

153.55
22,900
24,6
22,515,700
22,7,200
22,5,8
Bid
Offer
Vol
Low
1,017.90
368.00
368.0
36,421,00
6,454,00
0,435,00

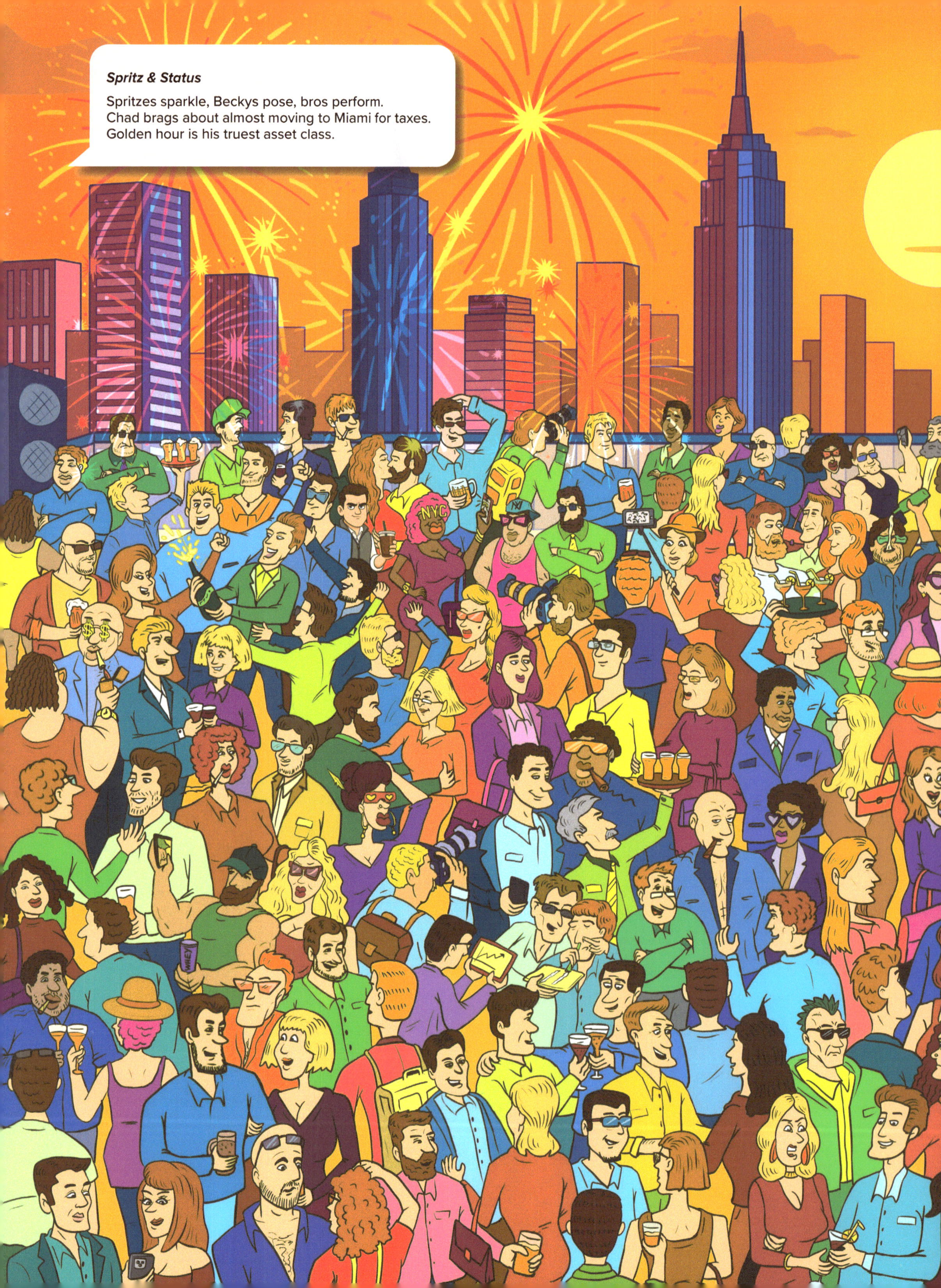

Spritz & Status
Spritzes sparkle, Beckys pose, bros perform.
Chad brags about almost moving to Miami for taxes.
Golden hour is his truest asset class.

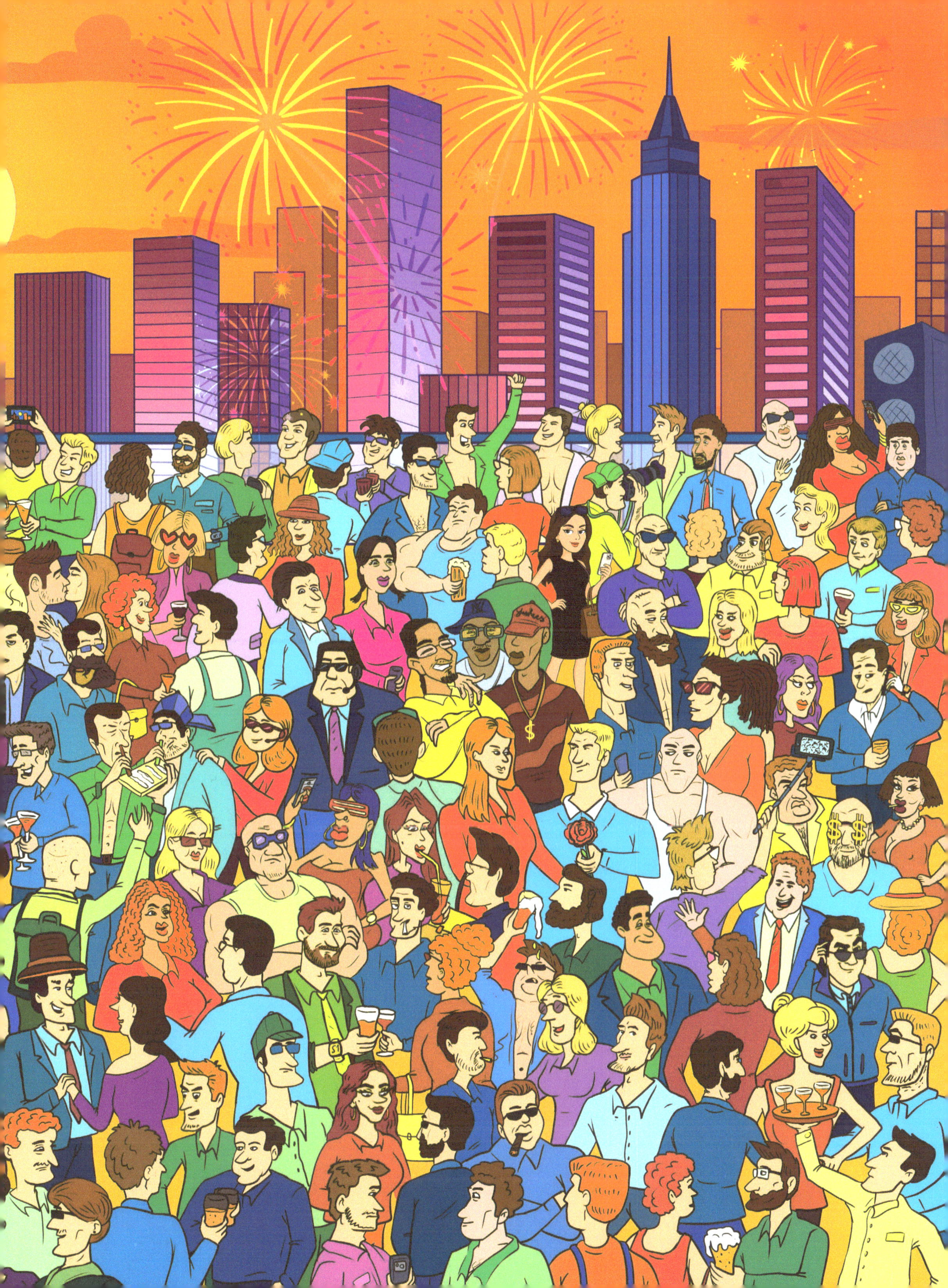

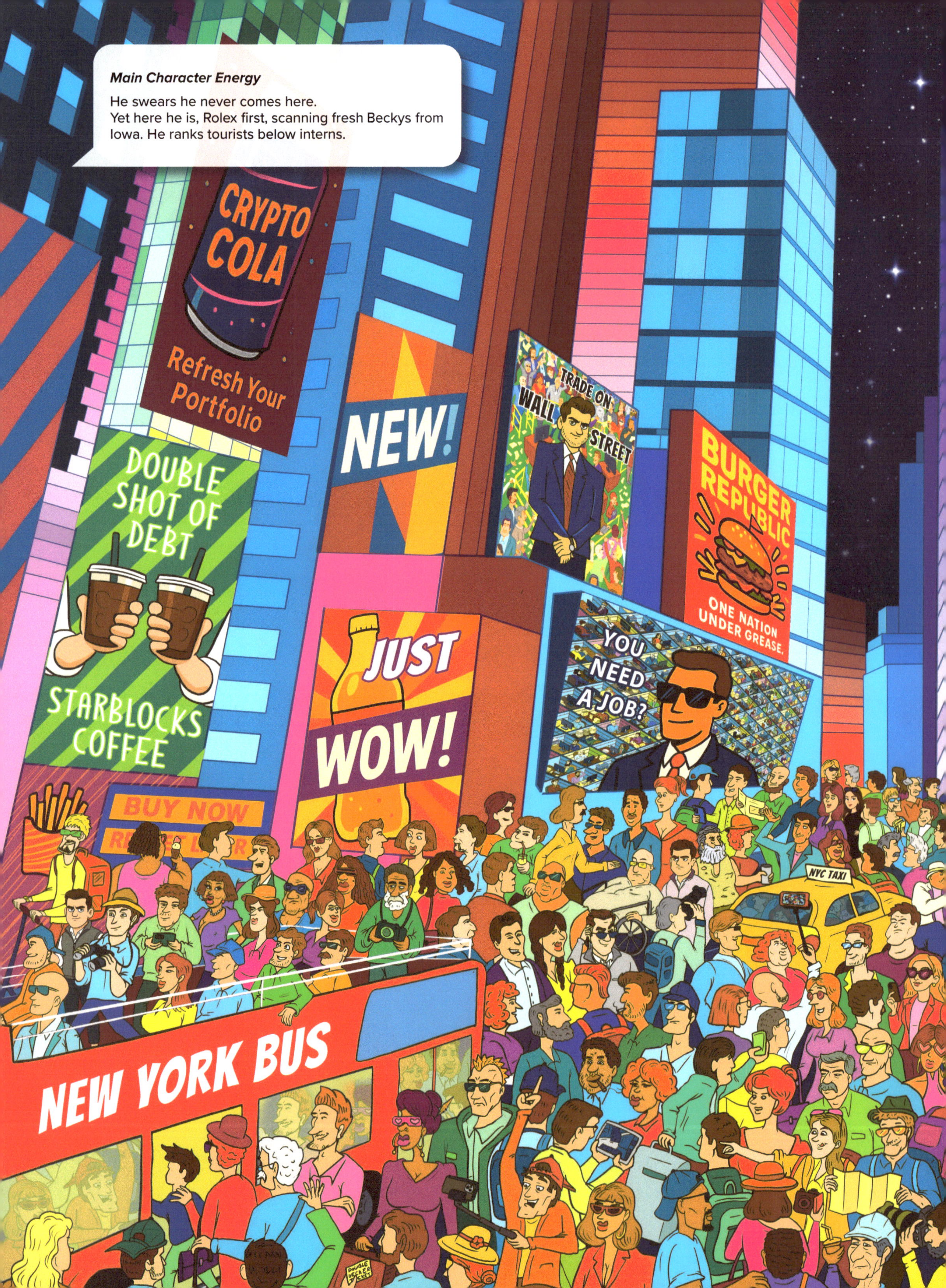
Main Character Energy
He swears he never comes here.
Yet here he is, Rolex first, scanning fresh Beckys from Iowa. He ranks tourists below interns.
CRYPTO COLA
Refresh Your Portfolio
DOUBLE SHOT OF DEBT
STARBLOCKS COFFEE
BUY NOW
NEW!
JUST WOW!
TRADE ON WALL STREET
YOU NEED A JOB?
BURGER REPUBLIC
ONE NATION UNDER GREASE.
NYC TAXI
NEW YORK BUS

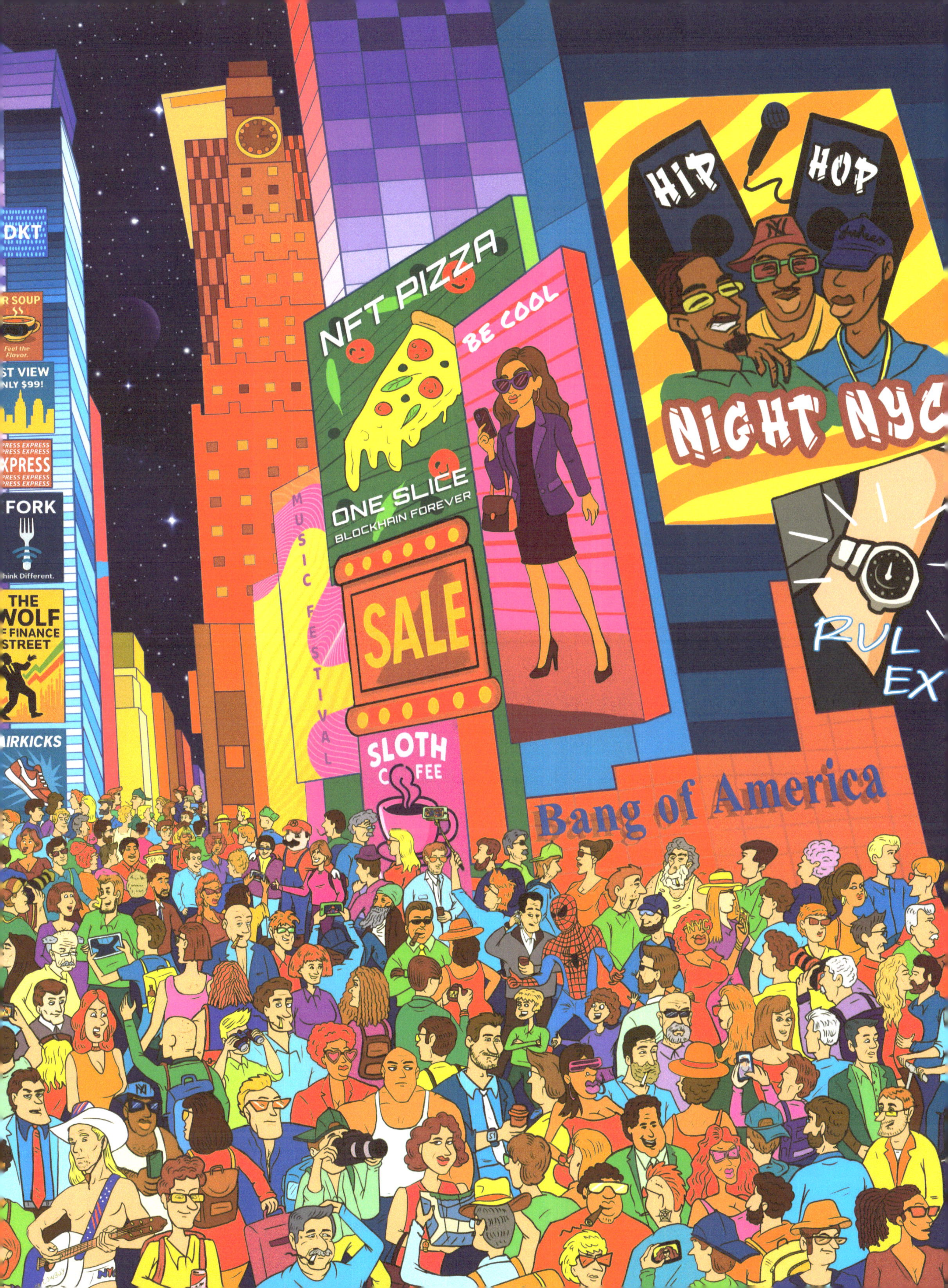

DKT
R SOUP
Feel the Flavor.
ST VIEW
NLY $99!
PRESS EXPRESS
XPRESS
PRESS EXPRESS
FORK
hink Different.
THE
WOLF
F FINANCE
STREET
IRKICKS
NFT PIZZA
BE COOL
ONE SLICE
BLOCKHAIN FOREVER
SALE
MUSIC FESTIVAL
SLOTH
COFFEE
HIP
HOP
NIGHT NYC
RVL
EX
Bang of America

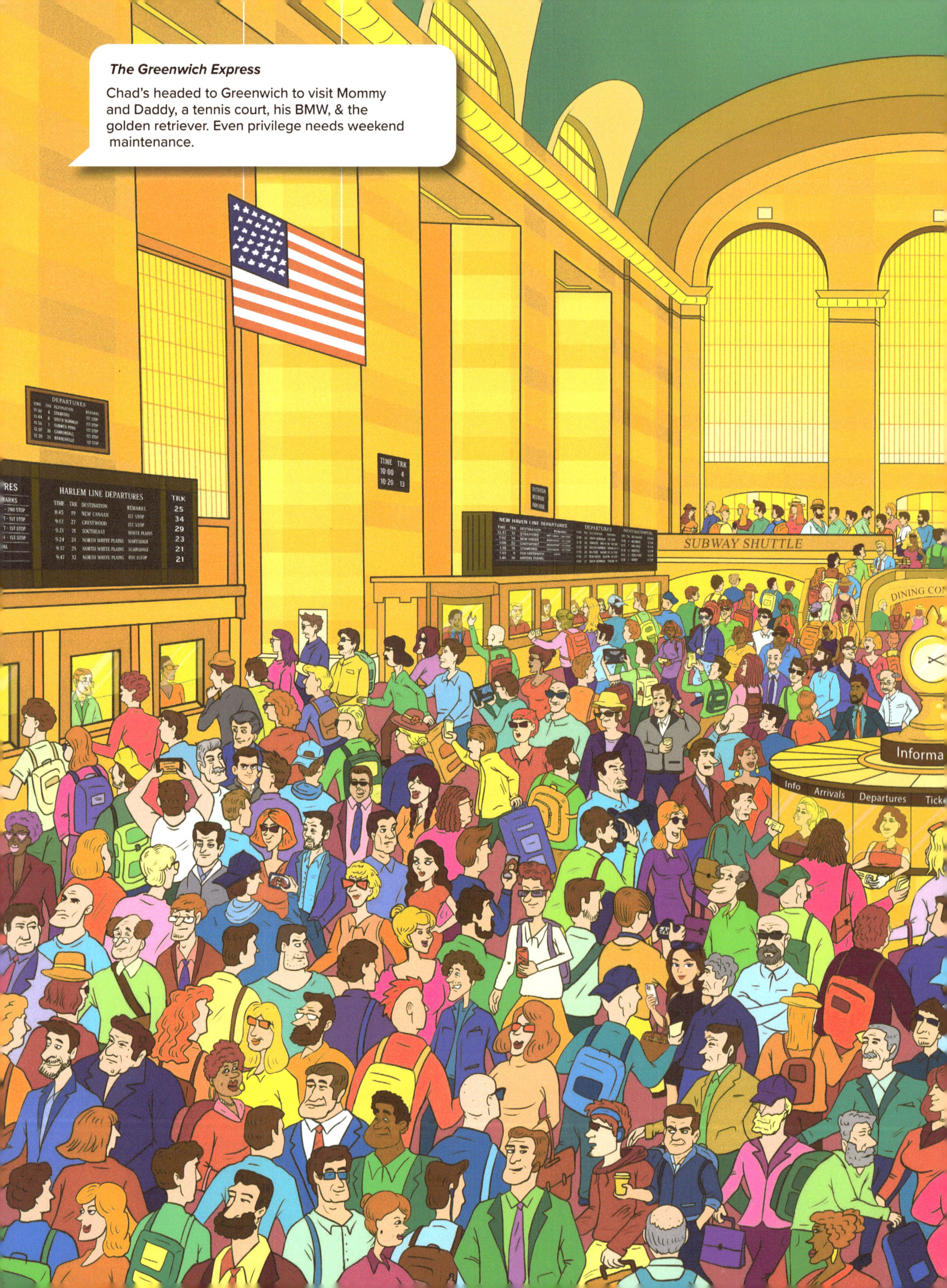

The Greenwich Express
Chad's headed to Greenwich to visit Mommy and Daddy, a tennis court, his BMW, & the golden retriever. Even privilege needs weekend maintenance.
SUBWAY SHUTTLE
DINING CO
Information
Info   Arrivals   Departures   Ticke
DEPARTURES
HARLEM LINE DEPARTURES
NEW HAVEN LINE DEPARTURES
DEPARTURES

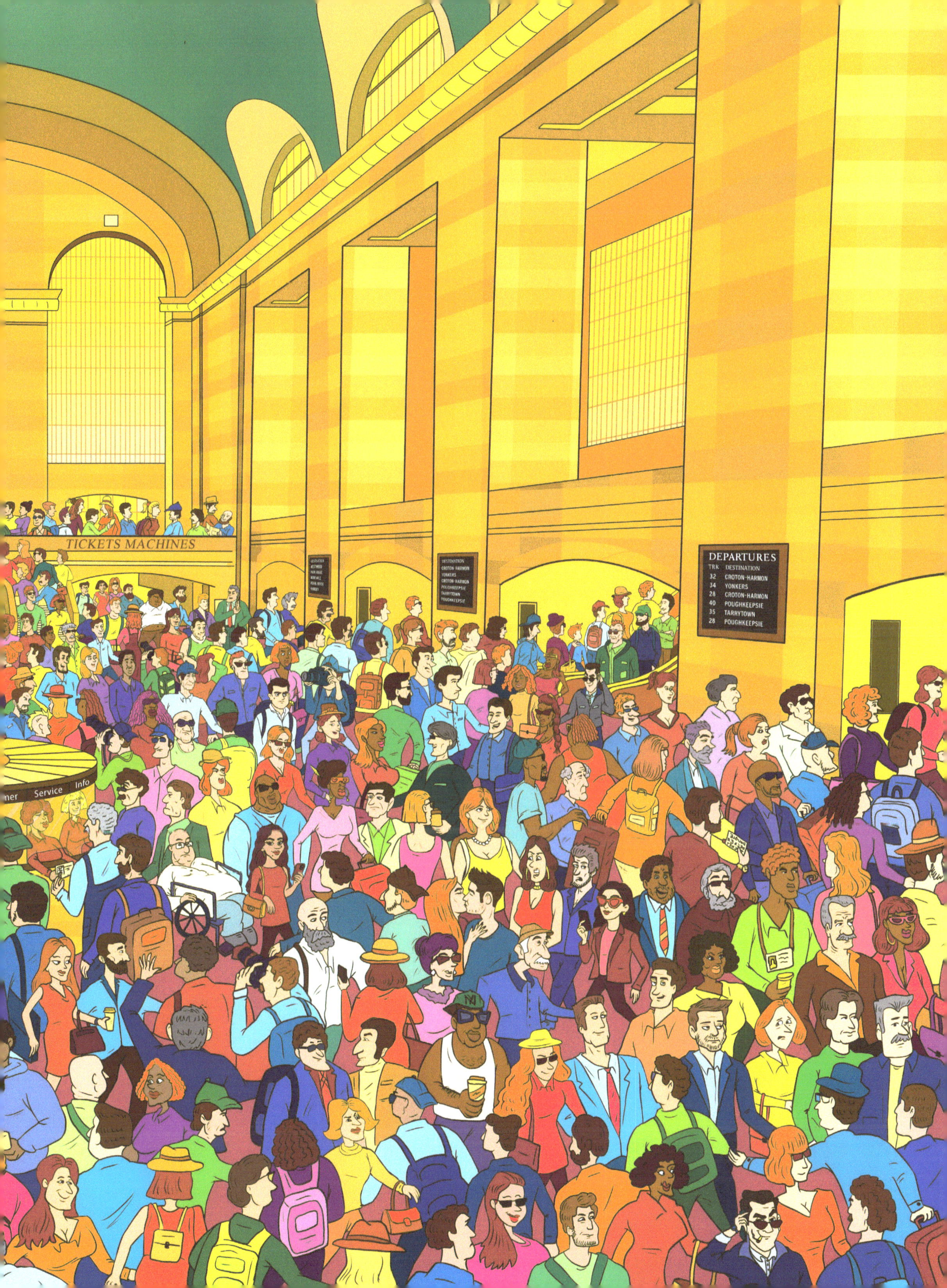

TICKETS MACHINES
...ner Service Info
DEPARTURES
TRK DESTINATION
32 CROTON-HARMON
34 YONKERS
28 CROTON-HARMON
40 POUGHKEEPSIE
35 TARRYTOWN
28 POUGHKEEPSIE
DESTINATION
CROTON-HARMON
YONKERS
CROTON-HARMON
POUGHKEEPSIE
TARRYTOWN
POUGHKEEPSIE

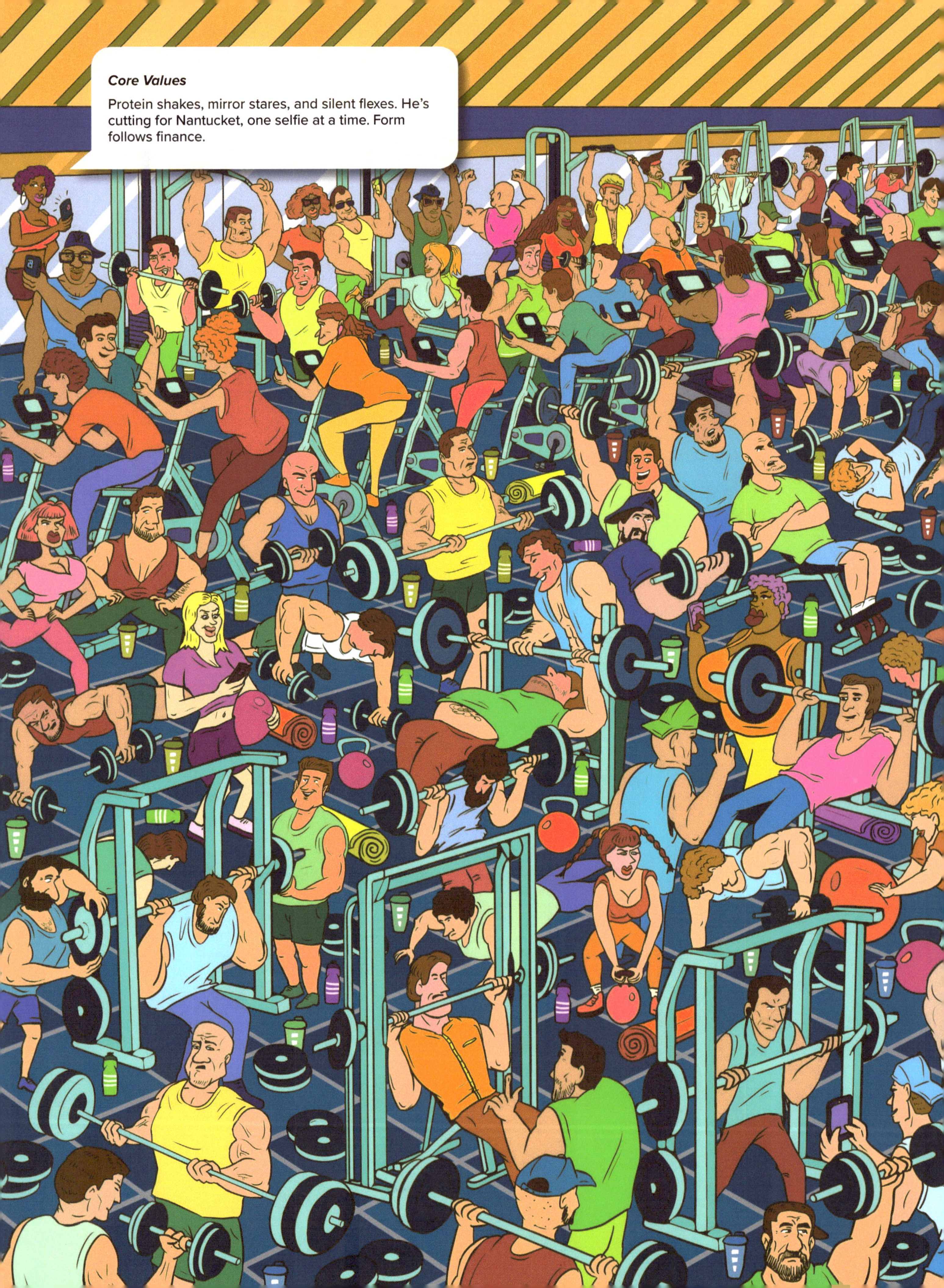
Core Values
Protein shakes, mirror stares, and silent flexes. He's cutting for Nantucket, one selfie at a time. Form follows finance.

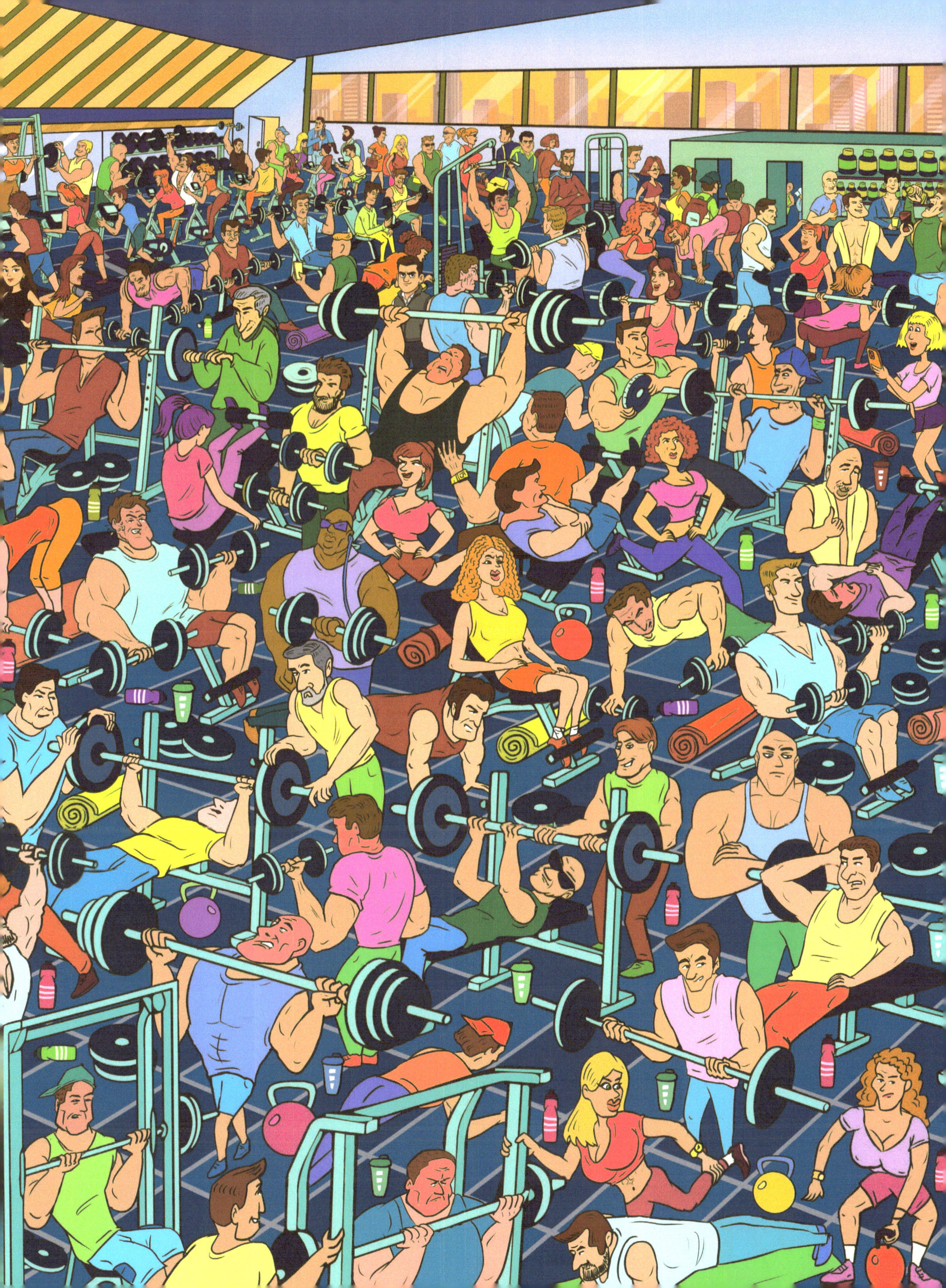

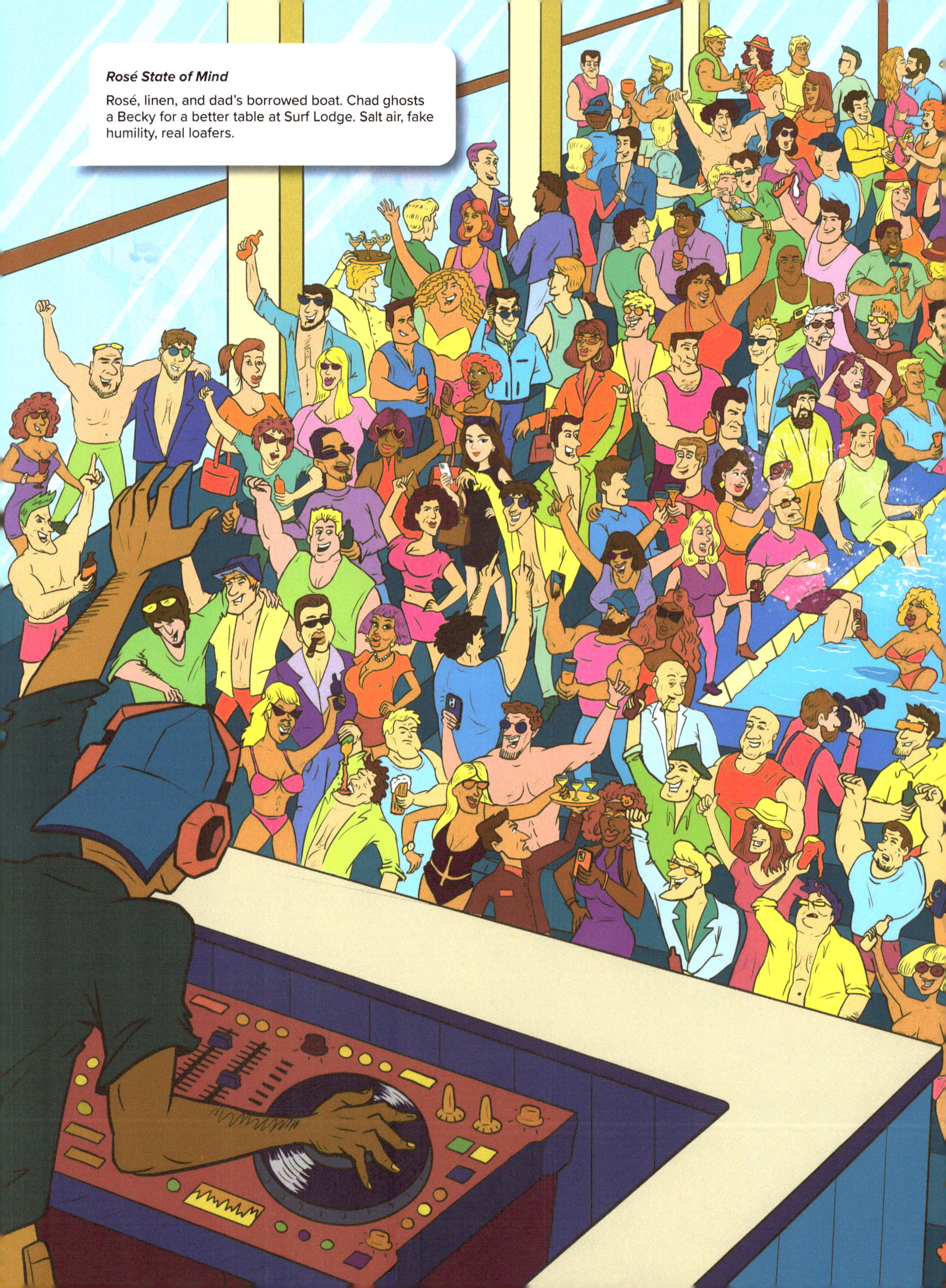

Rosé State of Mind

Rosé, linen, and dad's borrowed boat. Chad ghosts
a Becky for a better table at Surf Lodge. Salt air, fake
humility, real loafers.

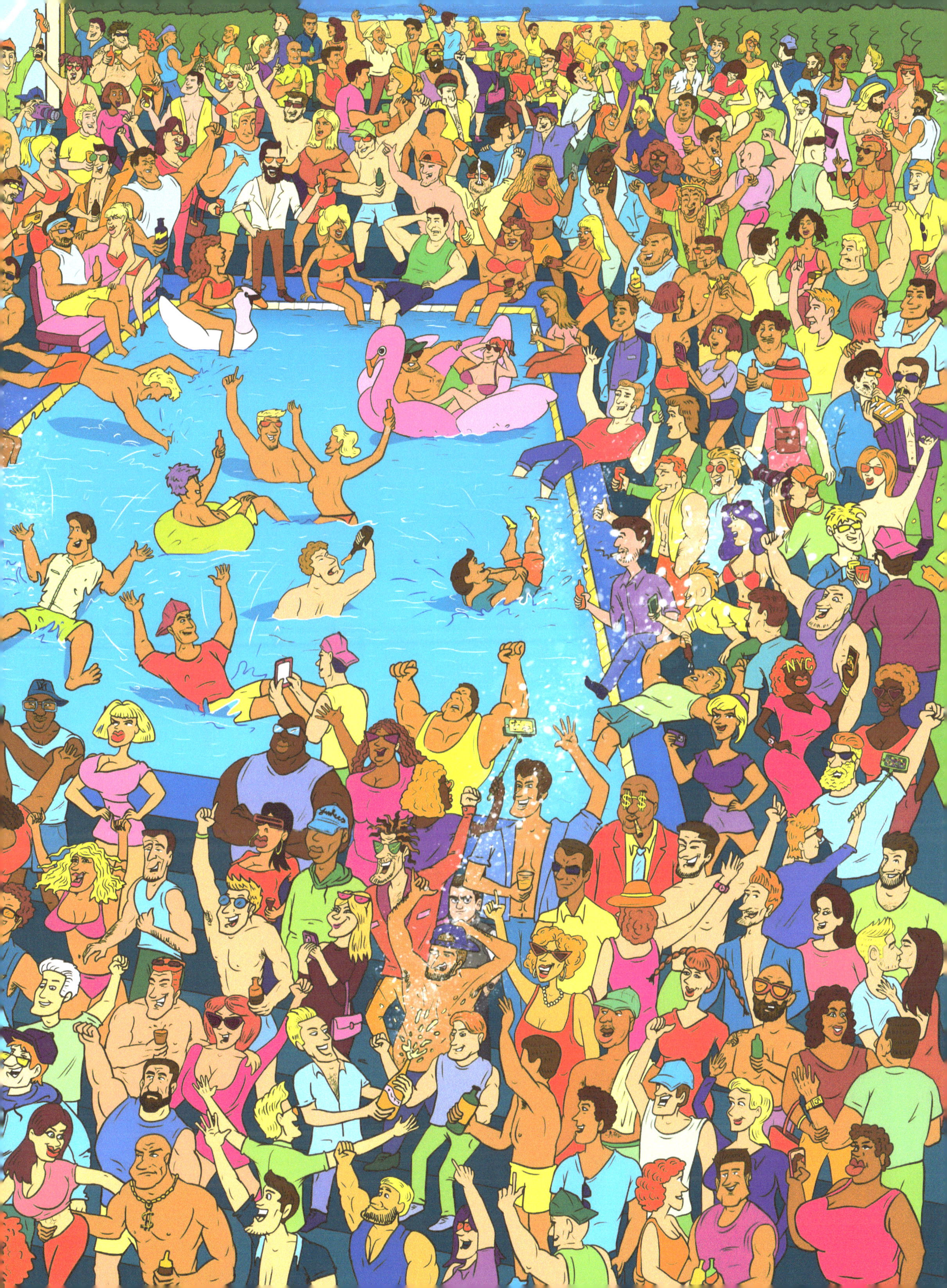

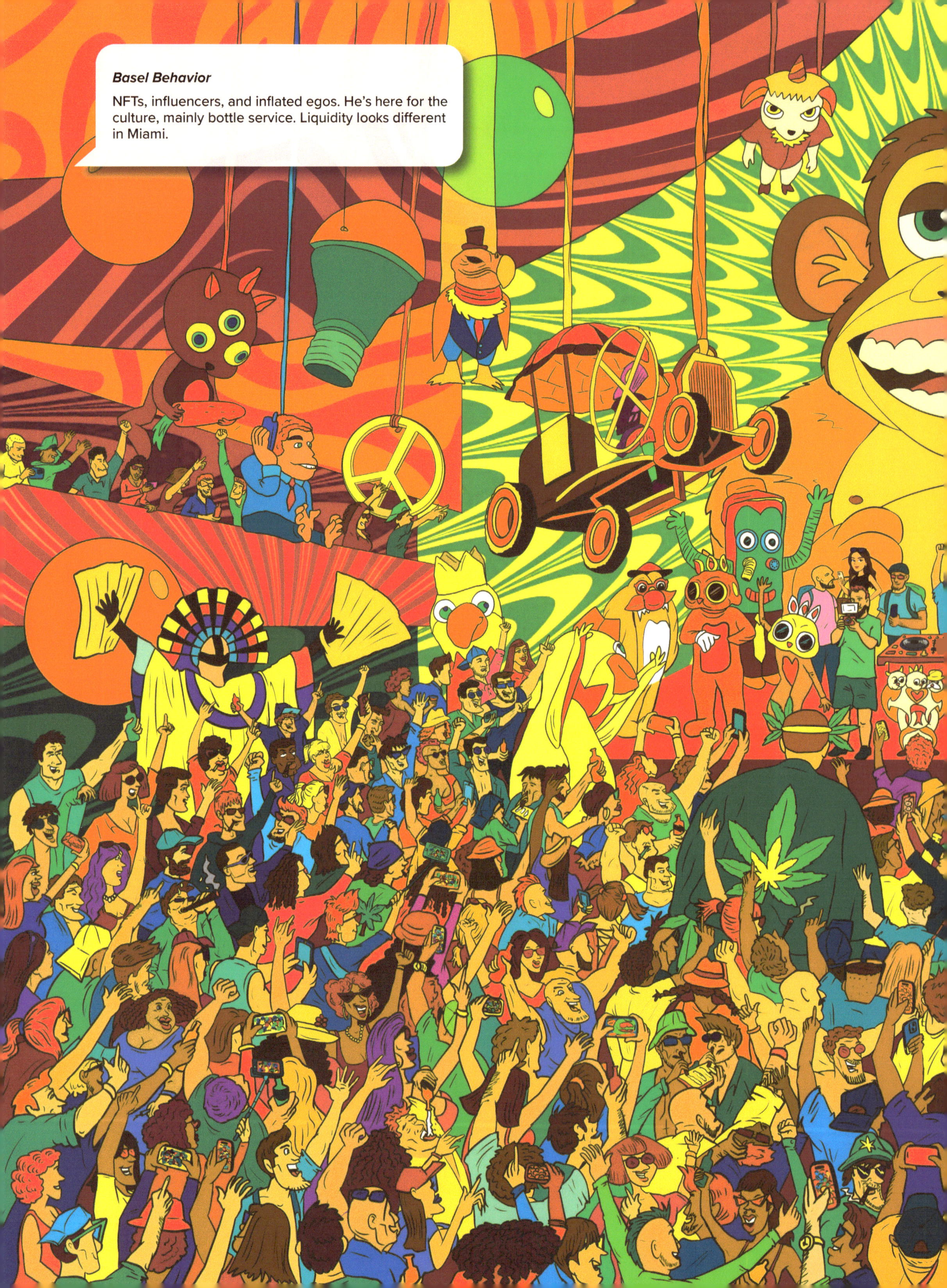

Basel Behavior
NFTs, influencers, and inflated egos. He's here for the culture, mainly bottle service. Liquidity looks different in Miami.

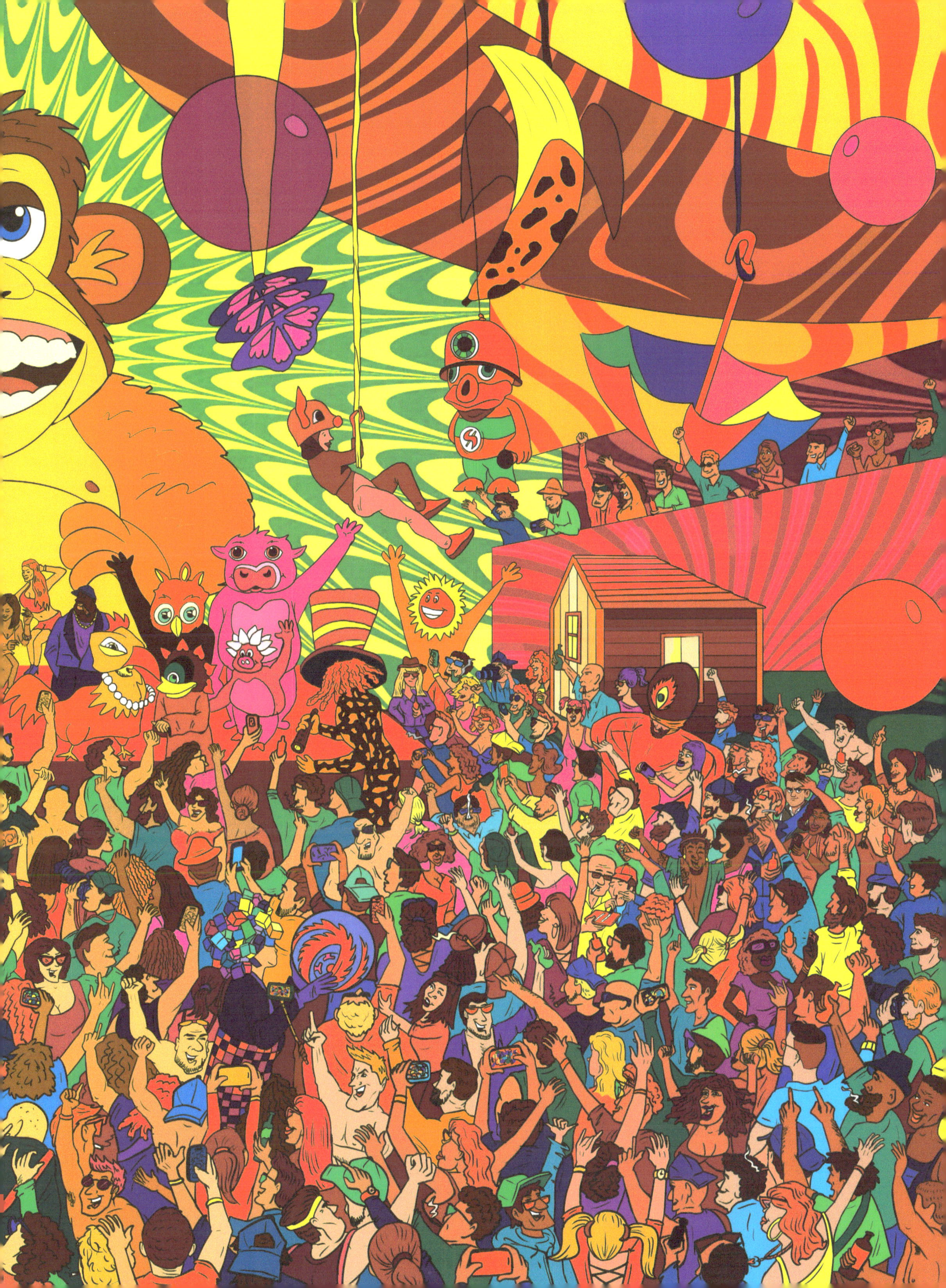

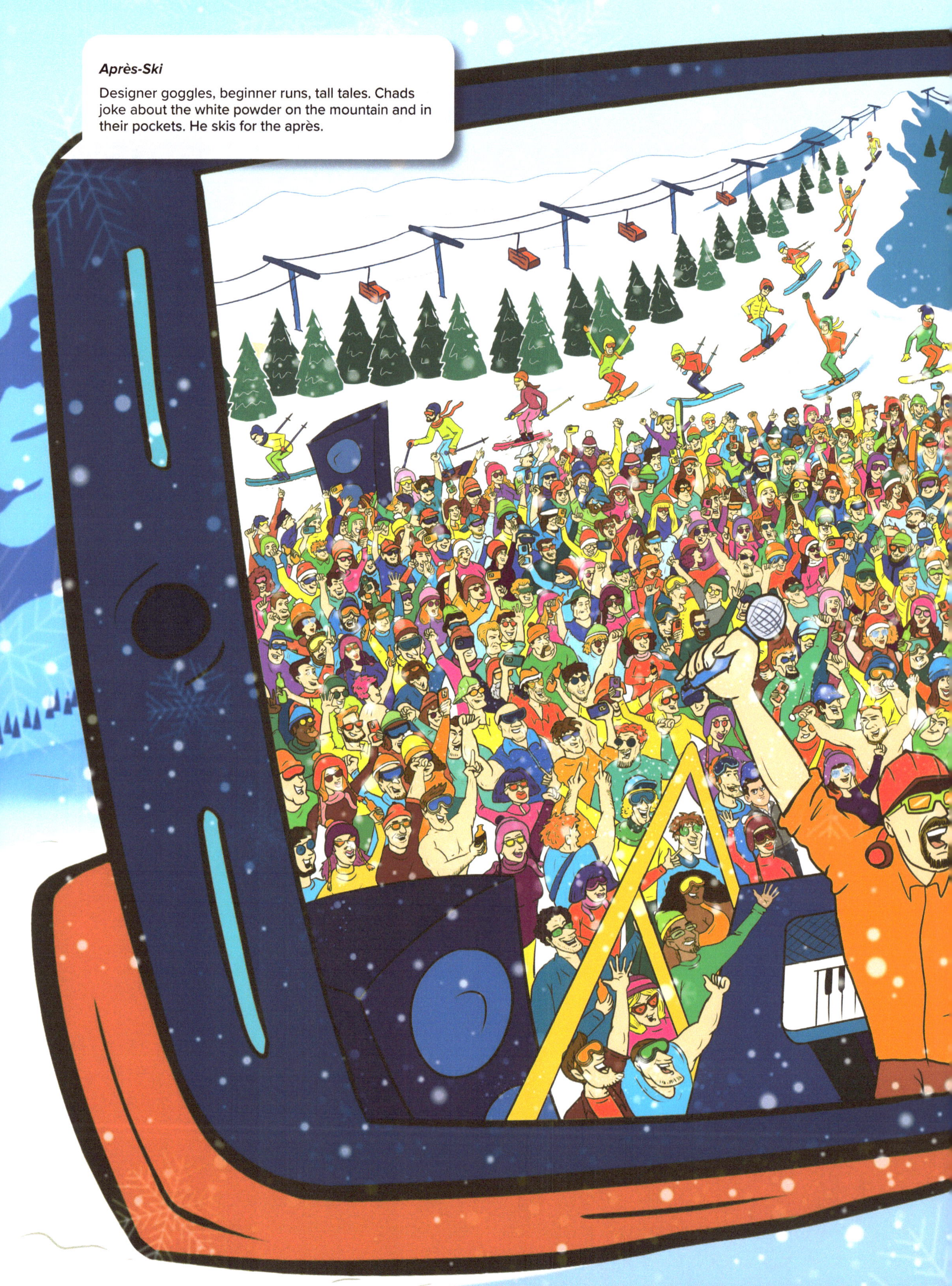

Après-Ski
Designer goggles, beginner runs, tall tales. Chads joke about the white powder on the mountain and in their pockets. He skis for the après.

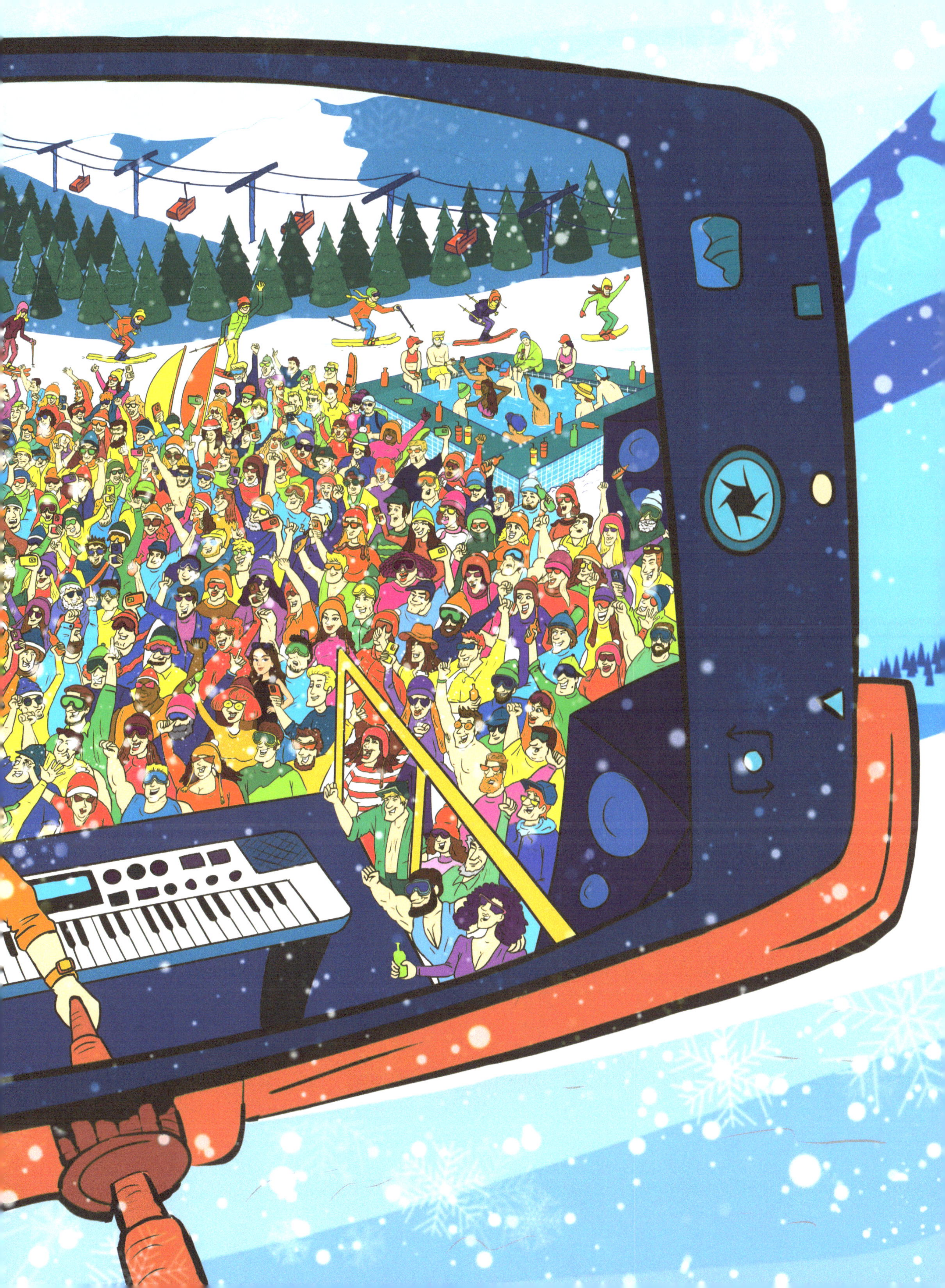

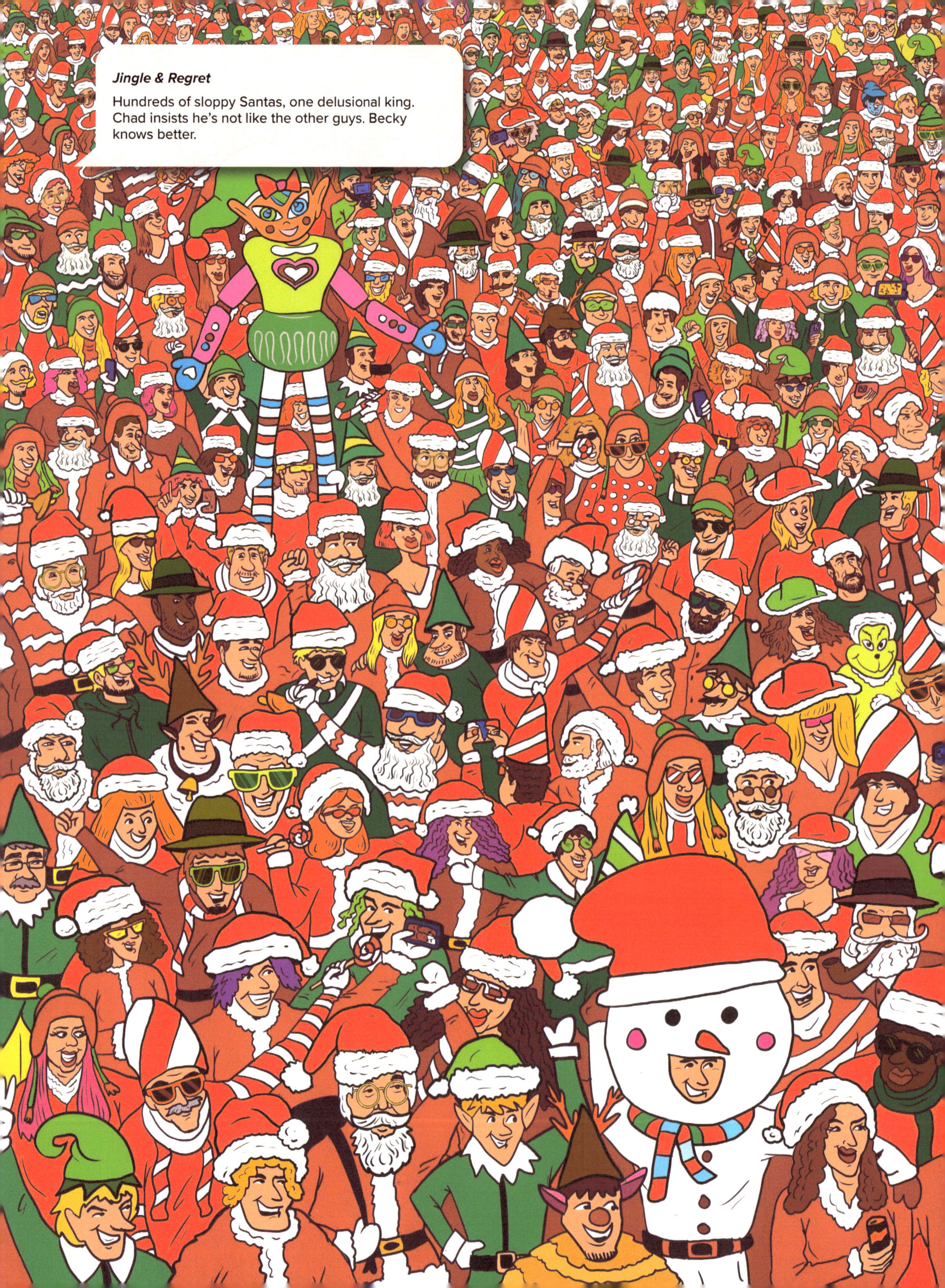

Jingle & Regret
Hundreds of sloppy Santas, one delusional king. Chad insists he's not like the other guys. Becky knows better.

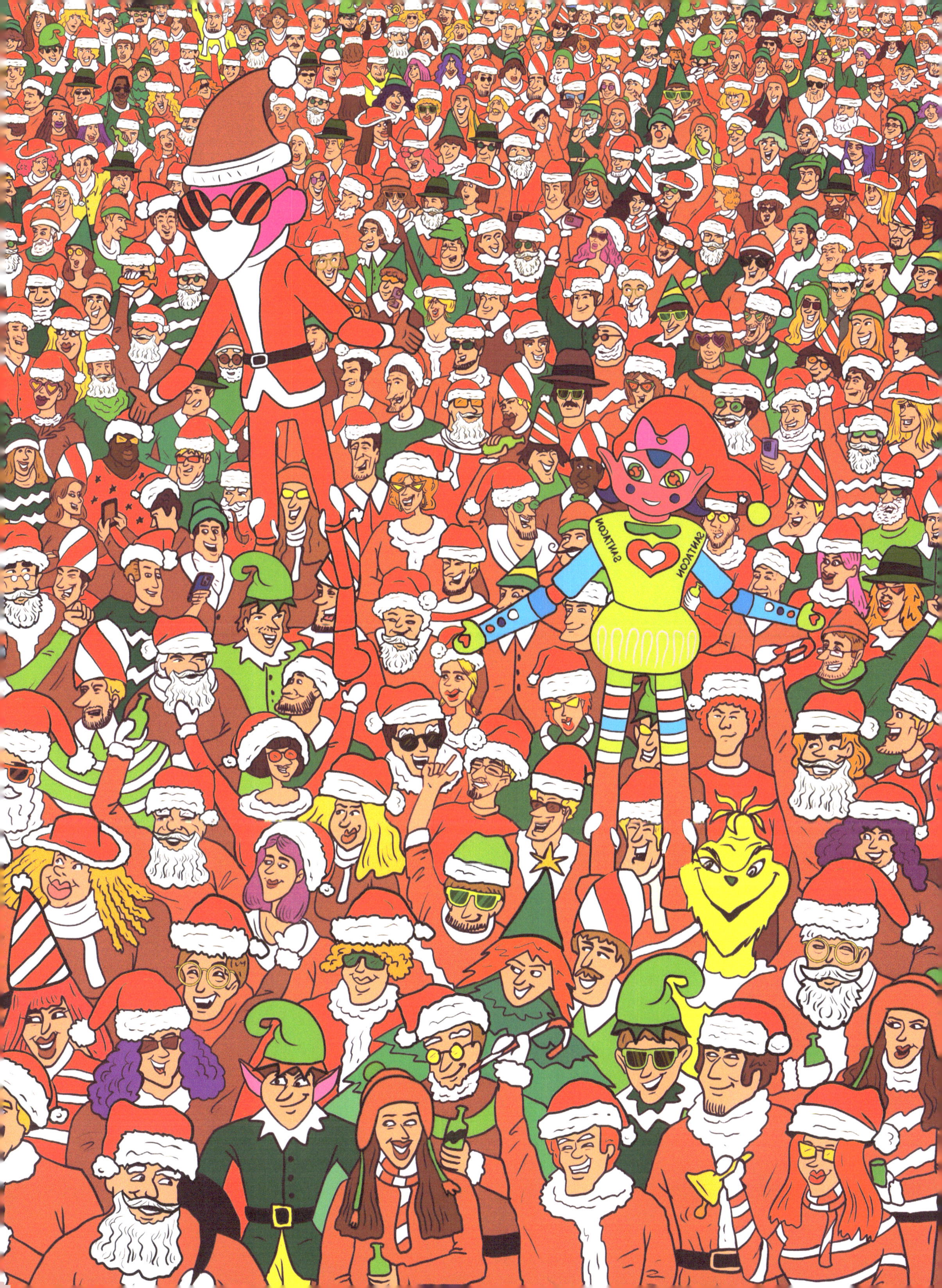

SANTACON
SANTACON

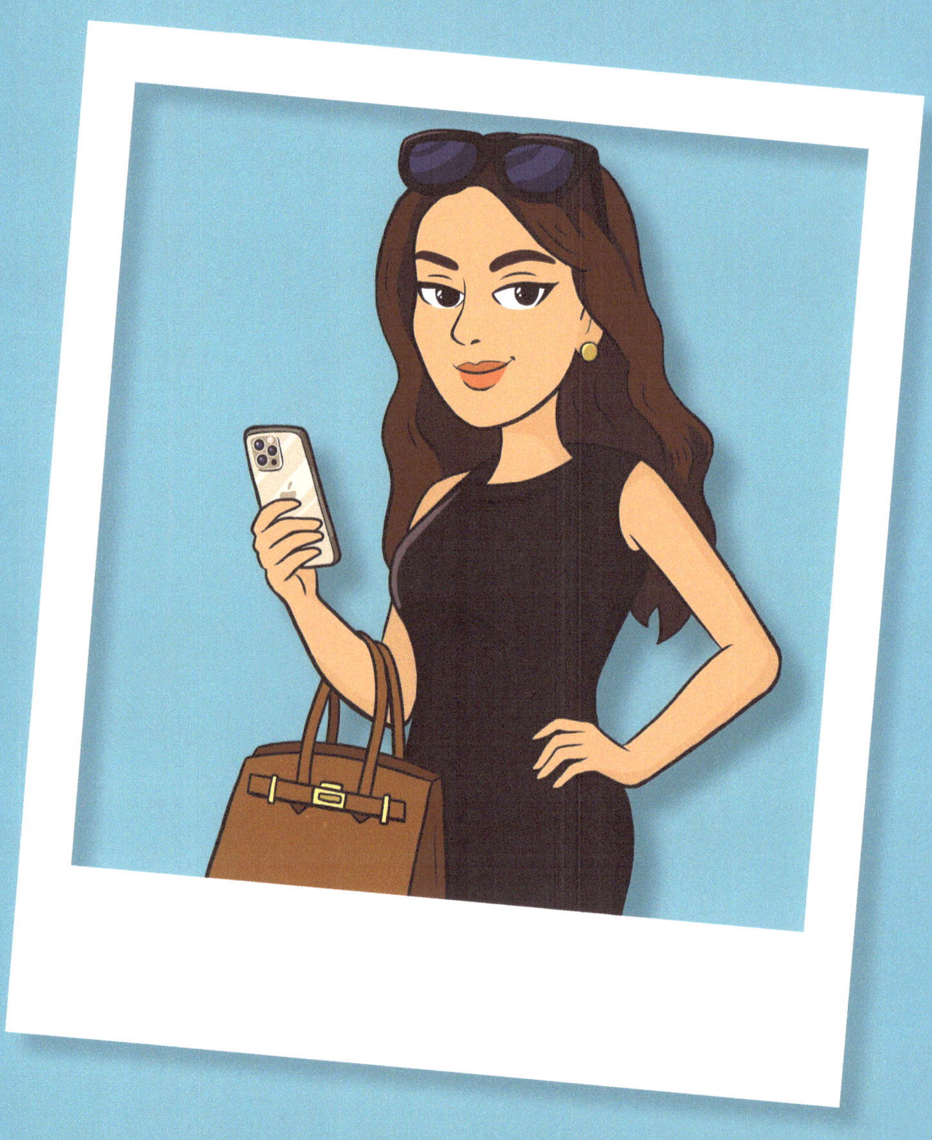

Where's Becky? (Spring 2026)

She's got Cartier bags, a sharper eye than Chad, and zero patience for finance bros. Can you find Becky before Chad does?

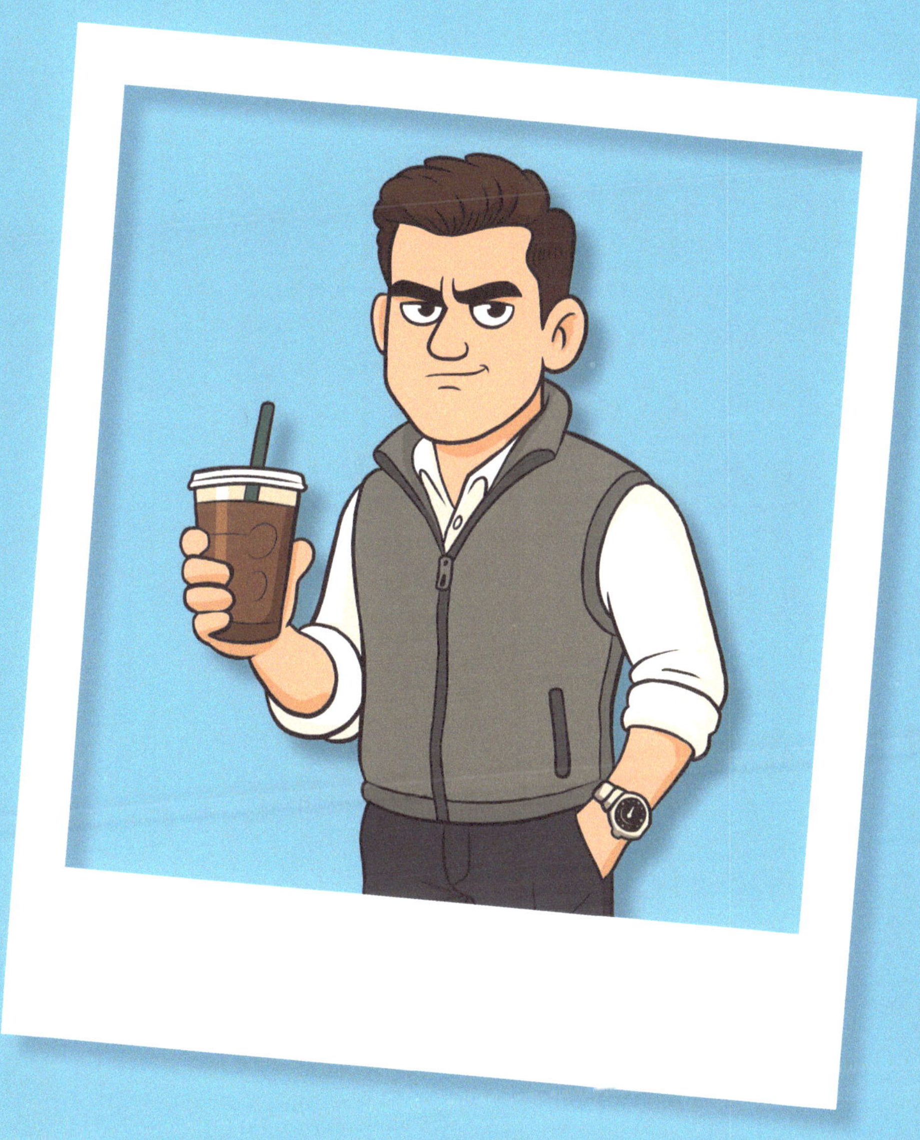

Where's Chad? Abroad (Late 2026)

From Mykonos beach clubs to Tokyo rooftops, Dubai deserts to London pubs — Chad thinks the world is his LinkedIn banner. Can you still spot him in the global chaos?